HOW TO BEAT THE ODDS TO YOUR GOAL

HOW TO BEAT THE ODDS TO YOUR GOAL

Robert Peprah-Gyamfi

Perseverance Book

HOW TO BEAT THE ODDS TO YOUR GOAL

All Rights Reserved. Copyright © 2017 Robert Peprah-Gyamfi

No part of this book may be reproduced or transmitted in any form or by any means, graphic, electronic, or mechanical, including photocopying, recording, taping or by any information storage or retrieval system, without the permission in writing from the copyright holder.
Published by Perseverance Books

For information please contact:
Perseverance Books, P.O.Box 8505,
Loughborough, LE11 9BZ, UK

www.peprah-gyamfi.com

ISBN: 978-0-9570780-7-9

"The heights by great men reached and kept, were not attained by sudden flight, but they, while their companions slept, were toiling upward in the night."

Henry Wadsworth Longfellow

TABLE OF CONTENTS

PREFACE xi
INTRODUCTION LIFE IS WAR xiii

PART ONE FACTORS WE SHOULD CONSIDER WHEN SETTING OUR GOAL.. 1

1) WHY DO WE WANT TO BE WHAT WE WANT TO BE?...3
2) ARE OUR MOTIVATIONS RIGHT? 7
3) ARE WE SUITABLE FOR THE TASK? 10
4) ARE WE SETTING ACHIEVABLE GOALS?...................12

PART TWO WORKING TOWARDS OUR GOAL 13

5) GOALS ARE NOT ATTAINED BUT ACHIEVED THROUGH HARD WORK 15
6) ADOPTING THE RIGHT STRATEGY COULD BE YOUR KEY TO SUCCESS...18
7) LET'S AIM HIGH AND EVEN HIGHER 20

PART THREE CHALLENGES ON OUR WAY TO OUR GOAL 23

8) LET'S GEAR OURSELVES FOR HARDSHIPS AND SETBACKS! 25
9) DEALING WITH UNEXPECTED TWISTS AND TURNS 27
10) LET'S KEEP ON EXPLORING FEASIBLE ALTERNATIVES RATHER THAN GIVE UP! 30
11) WHEN MISFORTUNE STRIKES, LET'S AVOID ENGAGING IN ENDLESS SELF-PITYING 35
12) AGAIN AND AGAIN WE MAY HAVE TO START AFRESH! 38
13) LET'S NOT BECOME TIRED OF KNOCKING ON EVERY DOOR THAT OFFERS HOPE OF PROGRESS 41
14) AS WE STRUGGLE TO MAKE IT, SOCIAL PRESSURE MAY MOUNT 43
15) LET'S NOT HANG ALL OUR HOPES ON OTHERS 45
16) WE MAY HAVE TO TAKE A GAMBLE ON THE FUTURE 47
17) IF ONLY FOR A WHILE WE MAY HAVE TO KEEP OUR PLANS TO OURSELVES 49
18) WE MAY BE FORCED TO SLEEP ROUGH AND ENGAGE IN DIRTY, BONE-BREAKING JOBS TO ACHIEVE OUR GOAL 50
19) UNEXPECTED EVENTS MAY SET IN TO THREATEN OUR PROGRESS 53
20) PROCRASTINATION IS THE THIEF OF TIME 56
21) WE MAY NEED TO TAKE A PLUNGE INTO THE DEEP UNKNOWN!! 58

22) SOME SEEMING MISFORTUNES MAY TURN OUT TO BE BLESSINGS IN DIGUISE..............................60
23) WE MAY NEED TO LEARN NEW SKILLS ALONG THE WAY 63
24) EVEN IN SEEMINGLY DEAD-END SITUATIONS – LET'S PERSEVERE STILL! 65
25) 'I DID NOT TRAVEL ALL THE DISTANCE FROM MPINTIMPI TO BERLIN TO GIVE UP!' 68
26) WE MAY NEED TO TEACH OURSELVES LATIN TO PROGRESS! 71
27) A HOSTILE ENVIRONMENT IS NO EXCUSE TO GIVE UP TRYING! 73
28) LET'S NOT BE BOTHERED BY WHAT OTHERS SAY OR THINK ABOUT OUR PLANS..........................75
29) EXPECT UNEXPECTED OPPOSITION 77
30) EVEN IN THE FACE OF ADVERSITY LET'S REMAIN FOCUSSED! 80
31) LET'S NOT SETTLE FOR MEDIOCRITY!!....................83
32) IF NEEDS BE, LET'S TA KE OUR CASE TO THE OBAMAS OF OUR TIME! 86
33) LET'S NOT ALLOW THE FAILURES OF OTHERS TO DISCOURAGE US 89

PART FOUR FINAL REFLECTIONS...............................93

34) ONE THING BEING ADMITTED TO MEDICAL SCHOOL: ANOTHER THING QUALIFYINGAS A DOCTOR ! 95
35) AS FAR AS IT DEPENDS ON US, LET'S BE ON GOOD TERMS WITH ALL 97
36) LET'S BE WARY OF DISTRACTIONS!..........................99

37) OTHERS JUMPING ON OUR BANDWAGON
OF SUCCESS 102
38) SO HOW DO WE BEAT THE ODDS
TO SUCCESS? 105

PREFACE

I HAVE KNOWN Dr Peprah-Gyamfi for a number of years now, ever since he published his first of many books, his autobiography called *The Call That Changed My Life*. Since then we have worked together on many projects, perhaps the most interesting and rewarding being when I had the privilege to interview him for a series of broadcasts on the Revelation TV channel. What impressed me so much about Dr Peprah-Gyamfi is his humility and gentle loving kindness in spite of his impressive achievements as a medical doctor, in Germany and the United Kingdom. His story, retold succinctly in this volume, is an impressive and amazing one, and will undoubtedly benefit many young persons setting out in life with dreams of success who might feel daunted, perhaps, by a disadvantaged background, lack of finances, and by the prospect of seemingly insurmountable hurdles that might lie before them.

There is a well-known saying, a cliché perhaps, that says, 'Where there is a will there is a way!' Dr Peprah-Gyamfi's account of his journey to success in the pages that follow without doubt prove the veracity of that statement! Born in a poor regional village in Ghana to working class parents who eked out their living from the soil they farmed, parents who could certainly not afford to send their son to a university in Europe when the opportunity was denied him in his native Ghana, the young boy never failed to cling to his dream of becoming a medical doctor. His perseverance in the face of disadvantages – a severe illness that handicapped his school-going years – and his resourcefulness in finding an alternative way that took him to toil as a labourer, in spite of his poor physique at the time, on building sites in Nigeria, is mind-blowing. Each hurdle led to a new step in achieving his goal. The final stages of that journey are equally amazing, when he encountered resistance in East and West Berlin, and faced the threat of being deported back to Ghana; all this makes fascinating reading. Apart from the legal and political hurdles, there was also the new challenge of having to learn to speak and write the German language from scratch – the language that would be the means of instruction for his medical degree at a prestigious German university!

All this shows the young reader – indeed, any reader – what the ingredients are for success. The most important are having a firm goal, a belief in oneself, the ability to persevere in the face of obstacles and discouragements, and to work hard. In short, this is an excellent handbook to take with you in your life's journey – a handbook you can refer to again and again when you are faced with discouragement and are in need of a fresh dose of motivation!

Charles Muller
MA (Wales), PhD (London), DEd (SA), DLitt (UOF)

INTRODUCTION
LIFE IS WAR

A TWI saying has it that some are born onto mountain tops – they have no problem growing tall. There are, indeed, those of our race who, by dint of their parentage, heritage, or other favourable circumstances, are *born onto mountain tops* and can as a result look forward to *growing tall* in life.

Another saying has it that 'Life is war'. Life indeed can be described as a war, a series of battles one after the other. Hardly has one battle been overcome than another rears its ugly head.

In this book I will be sharing the insights I have gained in my own *life's war*.

Born into the most deprived settings imaginable on earth, I managed to make my way from my impoverished little village, Mpintimpi, in rural Ghana, all the way to the Hanover medical school in Germany.

My path was not eased by way of a government scholarship – a package consisting of free travel documents plus boarding, lodging, textbooks, and other expenses covering the whole duration of my studies.

Neither was it eased by way of the assistance of a generous German missionary who had earlier noticed me on the streets of my poor village as I played football, bare-footed, with my peers. Far from that...

Instead, the path that led to the attainment of my cherished goal of becoming a doctor, and using my profession to improve the lot of my people, was fraught with a catalogue of challenges, one after the other.

Though written for general readership, this account of my journey is meant in particular for the youth, the adolescent and the young adult – that group of young persons who either are about to set out on a life-journey devoid of parental supervision, or have just made that leap of faith.

The book does not claim to provide a magic formula for success. Every individual is different. Scientists tell us that apart from identical twins, each of us is endowed with a unique DNA constitution. In the same way that we have unique gene mapping, our experience in life will also be unique – that is true even for identical twins. This book is about my experience. Your experience, dear reader, certainly will be different.

Nevertheless, it is my hope that in keeping with the Twi saying, 'those that are behind learn from the steps of those who have gone before', my book will provide a guiding light – and for this reason my prayer is that this account of my experience will be a source of inspiration and motivation for the reader.

* * *

Before I delve any further into the task I have set myself, I would like first to give the reader a brief account of my early childhood.

I was born into a tiny village with the big name of Mpintimpi. The small settlement is situated about 150 kilometres to the north of Accra, Ghana's capital city.

According to my mother I was born in the small rectangular wooden structure that served as the family bathroom. It measured about one metre in length and eighty centimetres in width. The wooden wall rose to about a metre and half above ground level. At the top the structure was open to the free tropical skies. The floor was not cemented but covered with fine gravel.

Even before I had time to settle on the planet I had elected to visit, my life was almost cut short by a large boil that developed on the left side of my neck. I was barely a year old. Fortunately I survived at a time when everyone had almost given up on me.

I was the fifth child of my mother. All her children born before me were boys. After me came three girls – thus I grew up with seven sibling. That was not the complete picture, I should add. Father had married a second wife a few years before my birth. He had six children with my stepmother. Thus, in the end, father had 14 children to care for from his meagre income as a peasant farmer.

Neither my mother nor my father attended school. As father used to tell us, he had a burning desire to go to school. Unfortunately for my parents, their respective parents did not have the means to send them to school.

In this respect their children were more favoured than themselves. At the time their children reached school-going age, the government of the newly independent Ghana had introduced free and compulsory education for all children.

When I was about six years old I was sent to school. There was no school at Mpintimpi at that time – we had to walk to Nyafoman, a larger village about three times the size of Mpintimpi, situated about three kilometres to the north of our village.

When I got to Primary 5, all of a sudden, and for no apparent cause, my left ankle began to swell up. Initially the accompanying discomfort was bearable, permitting me to continue to walk to school. In time, however, the pain increased in intensity, to the extent that I had to stay away from school. The forced interruption in my education would last for two years.

This introduction is very abridged. Anyone wishing to read a more detailed account of my arduous journey from my little village all the way to the Hanover Medical School is recommended to read my book *Medical School at Last*.

PART ONE
FACTORS WE SHOULD CONSIDER WHEN SETTING OUR GOAL

1
WHY DO WE WANT TO BE WHAT WE WANT TO BE?

THOUGH I CANNOT PINPOINT exactly when I made up my mind to study medicine, the decision came quite early in my life.

The question that one may want to ask me then is: 'Why did you aspire to become a doctor? One might have expected you to follow in the footsteps of your parents and choose to become a peasant farmer.'

While not wanting to demean the trade of my parents, I wish to point out that tilling the land with primitive instruments under the scorching African sun was not their profession of choice. As I have already mentioned, both my parents were desirous of attending school. Circumstances beyond their control prevented them from doing so. Outspoken as she was on matters relating to justice and equal rights, mother, given the chance, would probably have ended up as a politician fighting for the rights of women.

With his sharp mind (he learnt the English and Twi alphabets on his own and through his own perseverance learnt to read), father, on his part, given the opportunity, could have achieved a high position on the academic ladder of his choice.

Having been given the opportunity my parents were deprived of, it is perhaps not surprising that their children should aim higher and, indeed, take advantage of the opportunity offered them to strive to progress further in life.

On the issue of my decision to become a doctor and not for example an engineer or architect, I can say that it was based mainly on my desire to help improve the lot of the local population, in particular, and the country at large in the area of health care.

Several factors, both personal and non-personal, shaped my decision. I will cite the non-personal factors to begin with.

The widespread poverty of the inhabitants, combined with the fact that the nearest hospital was quite a distance from our village, led to the situation whereby the sick were usually kept in the village until the condition they were afflicted with reached advanced stages before efforts were undertaken to take them to hospital – in some cases it turned out too late for them to be helped.

When at long last extended family members managed to gather sufficient funds to enable the sick to be sent to hospital, the means of transport became an issue. The village happened to be located on a road linking two district capitals. Every morning about half a dozen vehicles travelling in both directions passed by. Often there were no seats or only a couple of seats left by the time they got to the village.

Though the general situation influenced my decision to study medicine, a few specific instances helped sharpen my decision further.

One day, as we walked home from school, four people carrying someone on a makeshift stretcher emerged from a bush path that linked some of the surrounding farmlands to the main road. As we learnt from them, the man they were carrying had been bitten by a snake whilst working on his farm about one kilometre away. After tying a rope some distance to the affected site on his left leg as a tourniquet, they decided to carry him to the main road in the hope that they would find a vehicle that would transport the injured man to the hospital about 30 kilometres away. Our ways parted, for we were heading in different directions. To this day I have wondered whether he ever made it to hospital. And if he did, was it too late for the doctors to save him?

Once a young resident of the village, a girl aged about ten years, sustained a deep machete wound to her right thigh whilst helping her parents at home! As blood oozed profusely from her blood vessels, the alarmed villagers instinctively tied a cord firmly above the wound in a desperate attempt to stop or at least to minimise the loss of blood. After waiting a few hours for the means of transport to take her to hospital, a vehicle eventually turned up. Happily, in the end, she was saved.

Then there was the case of Manu, my younger sister, who nearly succumbed to an attack of measles. For a while, due to lack of funds, my parents were unable to send her to hospital. In the meantime she became so emaciated, she looked literally like a living skeleton. In the end my parents managed to raise a loan to bring her to the attention of the doctors. The fact that she survived, for me, was miraculous.

A detailed account of all the medical crises, emergencies and problems I witnessed in and around our little settlement at the time I was growing up there would fill a large book. Before I proceed to another topic, however, I would like to tell readers about one scary incident that involved my mother.

Though she was not feeling well one day, the need to replenish the depleted food store of the family led to her decision to visit one of our farms to harvest foodstuff for the family. I was about ten years old at the time and was the only person who accompanied her on that occasion. In the course of our walk back home from the farm, her condition deteriorated to the point that I feared she would collapse in front of me. That she managed to make it home, still carrying on her head the load of food provisions she had fetched, is a real marvel. Just as she reached the perimeters of the compound of our home, she collapsed and fainted.

It took a while before we could find a vehicle to convey her to the hospital. Fortunately she made a complete recovery.

Added to the non-personal factors outlined above was my personal suffering with my left ankle. During the first two years of my affliction, I was subjected to a catalogue of horrible treatment 'remedies' from one traditional healer after the other. Despite the torture, no one could tell me exactly what the cause of my affliction was. In the end I firmly made up my mind to become a doctor, not only to help others, but also to understand what was behind the problem that had caused me so much suffering and misery.

2
ARE OUR MOTIVATIONS RIGHT?

THIS LEADS ME to the issue of motivation. What lies behind our decision to strive to attain a certain goal in life – to learn a trade, to pursue a degree course, or to choose a specific career?

Whatever the driving force that leads us to select a career or profession, our primary consideration should not be the wealth, privilege, prestige, fame, or power associated with the career, job, or degree we are striving to pursue or attain. The position we strive for may indeed bring with it the ancillary advantages touched upon, of wealth and prestige, for instance, but these considerations should not be our main driving force.

It is no secret that in some areas of the globe, some enter into politics with the sole aim of attaining power and influence, of personal prestige, and use those privileges to amass wealth, not only for themselves but also for their family members, friends, concubines, etc. This should however not be the driving force. Ideally one should seek a position or goal in life that will enable one to serve society and bring about an improvement in living conditions.

We should also be wary of choosing a profession just to please others – our parents, spouse, friends, peers, etc. Parents have the tendency to want their children to go in specific professional directions – to become doctors, dentists, engineers, architects, etc.

In these days, when top stars in sporting fields such as football, rugby, tennis, motorsports, or basketball earn fortunes, parents may also be inclined to direct their children into such areas of human endeavour even though they may not be endowed with the requisite talents.

I am not saying or implying that parents should not offer their children guidance in their career aspirations. They should, however, desist from imposing their wills on them.

For example, the fact that they failed to achieve their aspiration to become so-and-so in life does not imply they should force their offspring to, as it were, 'catch-up' on their missed opportunities.

Also, the fact that the neighbour's children are excelling in a certain field of human endeavour should not cause parents to engage in a kind of competition with them by directing their children into that field.

During my student days in Hanover I used to work occasionally as a translator for various bodies – the police, immigration authorities, the courts, etc. I still remember the translation I did in the case of a young woman from Ghana who had been arrested trying to enter the country with a fake passport of the Ivory Coast, Ghana's immediate neighbour to the west.

In the event, it came to light that she herself had no interest at all in travelling to Europe. The decision was instead forced on her by her parents. They wanted her to be like their neighbour's children who were already settled in Europe. In the event they paid money to a 'connection man', to arrange her journey to Europe. Having successfully helped her to Europe, she was eventually abandoned to find her own way in the strange environment. Left alone, she was completely at a loss to know what to do in what for her was an alien environment. It came as no surprise to me when I got to know about her background. She dropped out of school at the primary school level. Up until the time she left her little village, situated about 300 kilometres to the north east of the capital Accra to board her flight, she had never travelled outside of her familiar environment.

She was so naïve, raw and uniformed, she might even have got lost in Sunyani, the capital of the region of her birth. How her parents could have decided to spend the income earned from harvesting their cocoa beans to sponsor her to Europe amazes me to this day.

In the end she pleaded with the authorities to send her back home as soon as possible – which they did.

3
ARE WE SUITABLE FOR THE TASK?

WE MAY BE INTELLECTUALLY GIFTED to pursue a career, but are we emotionally equipped? We may dream of becoming a pilot – but if we have a fear of heights or a fear of flying, we would be well advised to look for something else. Though I do fly from time to time, I cannot imagine myself choosing flying as a profession.

We may want to study medicine; we may even be brilliant students capable of mastering the challenging course of study. If, however, we are frightened by the sight of blood, not able to cope with sights of horrific injuries, or being confronted by various forms of human suffering, for example emaciated children, dead bodies, etc., we would do well to reconsider our decision – unless we are prepared to end up in non-clinical fields that do not require direct contact with patients.

During my first year in medical school, we dissected dead bodies on a weekly basis as part of the anatomy lessons. On our very first exposure to corpses, one of our fellow students collapsed at the sight of the human remains and was led away – never to return.

We should not only have the interest and talent for a profession, or career; we should also be physically fit to pursue it.

Though I was a keen footballer, I did not consider myself talented. Apart from that, the trouble with my left ankle that began in my early teenage years left me physically unable to pursue any career requiring physical exertion.

4
ARE WE SETTING ACHIEVABLE GOALS?

WE MUST SET GOALS that are achievable. Was the goal of studying medicine achievable in the case of the son of a poor peasant farmer from little Mpintimpi?

The answer is that my chances of attaining that feat, though very remote, were not beyond the realms of what was possible.

Ghana at that point in time boasted only a single medical school (the number had increased to two by the time I applied). Not only was tuition free, students also did not have to pay for boarding and lodging. On top of that, there was a student loan scheme which would take care of my books.

The main problem lay in the annual intake of students. In those days the only existing medical school admitted only a handful of students annually. As might be expected, the competition was very keen. Nevertheless, I was prepared to face the challenge.

The situation would have been different had I aspired to become an astronaut. Even if I was personally suitable for the profession, the fact that Ghana did not have the requisite infrastructure would have made such a goal impossible to attain.

PART TWO
WORKING TOWARDS OUR GOAL

5
GOALS ARE NOT ATTAINED BUT ACHIEVED THROUGH HARD WORK

MY DESIRE to contribute to an improvement in the health care of my community was the main factor in my decision to study medicine.

How did I work towards the realisation of my goal?

As I mentioned earlier, my chances of making it to university were very slim indeed. Apart from my parents being poor and illiterate, the prevailing education system in those days placed children like myself attending the public elementary school at a great disadvantage. To give readers an idea of what I am driving at, I will pause to provide a brief overview of the educational system prevailing in Ghana at that time. Being a former British colony, it aligned its educational system with that of the former colonial power.

The educational system consisted basically of three cycles – the first being elementary school, the second being secondary school, and the third or tertiary cycle being university and other institutions of higher learning.

Elementary schools were spread throughout the country, and it took ten years for pupils to complete this cycle or primary level of education.

Unlike elementary schools, secondary schools were usually situated in large towns and cities – in district and regional capitals as well as in Accra, the national capital.

To make secondary school education accessible to children from areas that were deprived of them, the majority of them were run as boarding schools. Though tuition was free at every level of education, secondary school students had to pay for their board and lodging.

After five years in secondary school pupils had to sit for the GCE 'O'-Level (General Certificate of Education, Ordinary Level) examinations. Those who performed well could proceed to a further two-year course at the end of which they sat for the GCE 'A'-Level (Advanced Level) examinations. Three passes at the 'A'-Level could open the way for one to study in one of the three universities existing in the country at that time.

To have the chance of pursuing further education up to university level, one had first to make the leap from elementary school into secondary school. In order to do that one had to pass what was referred to as the common entrance examination – a nationwide assessment test.

The affluent and the rich usually avoided the public elementary school system when looking for schools for their children. Instead they sent them to special schools where pupils were groomed purposely to pass the common entrance examination. To allude to that fact, the schools became known as preparatory schools.

Was this because of poor tuition offered by the public elementary schools? Was it because they were not geared purposely towards passing the common entrance examination and instead provided broad elementary education? Whatever the reason, the fact was that the pass rate of candidates from the public elementary schools did not match the significantly higher pass rate of the candidates from the preparatory schools.

It was one thing wanting to take the examination; it was another getting someone to pay the examination fee. Though it amounted to 'peanuts' for the wealthy, it was beyond the means of many ordinary parents. Fortunately for me, my parents made the sacrifice and paid the registration fee.

It was one thing getting registered; it was another thing passing the examination. I did not leave anything to chance but sat down to seriously prepare for it. In the main it involved working through previous examination questions. My efforts were rewarded – out of about 40 candidates who took the test from my school, only I and another candidate were successful.

6
ADOPTING THE RIGHT STRATEGY COULD BE YOUR KEY TO SUCCESS

MY ADMISSION to secondary school gave me a great boost on my road to the realisation of my goal. It was important for me, though, not only to work hard academically, but also to select the right subjects.

At that time, a candidate wishing to be considered for admission to medical school was required to obtain three passes at 'A'-Level, two of which should be chemistry and physics. The third subject could be either biology or mathematics.

With my eyes fixed on my goal, I selected the right subjects at the GCE 'O'-Level in preparation for the sixth form. To be awarded the GCE 'O'-Level certificate, one had to obtain passes in English and mathematics. One also had to obtain good passes in the three subjects one was desirous of offering at the GCE 'A'-Level. With the above considerations in mind, I ended up offering the following subjects: English, mathematics, additional mathematics, chemistry, biology, physics, geography and economics.

I did not take chances when it came to preparing for an examination. The thought of cheating my way through my examinations never crossed my mind. Though the lights were switched off at 10pm at the boarding house, a great deal of those preparing for exams engaged in what was termed 'mining' – a situation where we stayed awake long past midnight making use of candles as the source of light.

7
LET'S AIM HIGH AND EVEN HIGHER

I AM NOT PROPOSING that we aspire to become engineers, architects, or pharmacists when we are struggling to attain passes at the secondary school level. As far as it is within our capabilities, however, I would urge you to aim high – indeed, to keep on aiming high.

When I sat for the common entrance examination, I selected Oda Secondary School, one of the few secondary schools in our district, in fact the pride of the Akim Kotoku district. My brother Ransford had been there – he urged me to do the same.

Moving from Mpintimpi to Oda was like moving from the dark jungle into the bright lights of the city.

Five years on, when I approached the end of my GCE 'O'-Level, I decided to aim higher and higher.

It was customary in those days, for those wishing to continue their education to the GCE 'A'-Level, to fill in forms to select their choices of school. One could choose three schools in order of preference. Not every secondary school offered sixth-form education. 'O'-Level leavers from such schools had no choice but to look beyond the boundary of their schools for suitable schools to apply to.

I did not need to face that problem since Oda Secondary School was a sixth-form school.

Still, I looked beyond the boundaries of Oda Secondary for my sixth-form school – to the disappointment of my teachers.

In the end I opted for Mfantsipim School in Cape Coast, a coastal city located about 100 kilometres to the west of Accra.

Built in 1876 by the Methodist Missionaries to the then Gold Coast, it prided itself as being one of the most prominent secondary schools in the country. A large number of famous people had passed through its walls.

It was a bold decision and not without risk. The school naturally would give preference to its own 'O'-Level candidates desirous of completing their further education there. Since it had become an elite school I expected to face, in addition, competition from the children of the rich and mighty of society who desired to move there from elsewhere for the sixth-form course. This meant the only way I could 'make it' there was to distinguish myself in the 'O'-Level examination.

Overflowing with self-confidence, I sought in my own small way to make a political statement, to the effect that the children of peasant farmers the likes of Kofi Gyamfi and Amma Owusuah of little Mpintimpi, given the chance, were capable of competing in the same league as the children of the affluent and powerful.

And so it transpired! Emerging as the best student of my year group at Oda Secondary School – the only candidate to pass out with Grade 1 distinction – Mfantsipim opened its doors to me in the academic year 1976–1977.

With my set goal before me, I selected physics, chemistry and biology at sixth-form level. Thus far, I was enjoying a jolly good ride towards my set goal... But, my dear reader, it was too early to congratulate me!

Towards the end of the two-year sixth-form course, those wishing to enter university – I did not come across anyone who did not – were required to fill in admission forms to one or more of the three universities available at that time. These were located in Accra, Kumasi and Cape Coast.

At the time I was growing up Ghana boasted only one medical school in Accra; at the time of filling in my university admission forms, Kumasi had not long opened a medical faculty. Between the two universities a total of about 80 students were admitted once annually.

As usual I left no stone unturned in my preparation for the 'A'-Level examination in May–June 1978.

As I put the final flourish to the last and final examination paper, I did not feel nearly as triumphant as I did two years earlier during the 'O'-Level examination. Nevertheless, I was reasonably confident I had done well enough to gain admission into one of the two medical schools.

And so, in this state of mind, I boarded a vehicle and headed home from Mfantsipim. I looked forward to being admitted to one of the two medical schools that October – if not into the well-established one in Accra, at least into the young faculty in Kumasi.

PART THREE
CHALLENGES ON OUR WAY TO OUR GOAL

8
LET'S GEAR OURSELVES FOR HARDSHIPS AND SETBACKS!

IN AN IDEAL WORLD we hope that what we plan to do will surely come to pass, in the way we planned it. If I desire to become an architect, and I have an interest in that field, and am also blessed with the talent of drawing, I may have reasonable expectations of success. Furthermore, let us assume that my parents were able to pay for my education – a promising prospect, we might think. And I may indeed end up realising my goal. I should however be prepared for unforeseeable events – personal, non-personal; man-made, natural, accidental, non-accidental, etc., that may set in to put my plans in disarray.

We should indeed gear ourselves to face disappointments, hurdles, obstacles, etc., events that impede our progress on our set course – not on one occasion, not on two, not on three, but indeed on several occasions!

We must in such situations guard ourselves against self-pity, avoid the 'why me?' attitude. For certainly, we would not be the only individual walking on the surface of the earth battling with the vicissitudes and challenges of life at any specific moment.

The reality is that burdens, hurdles, hardships, etc., are part and parcel of life. I have experienced them and continue to experience them first hand.

Is it poverty and want that constitute the main burden? Well, I certainly experienced them in abundance in little Mpintimpi. Is it personal suffering, like placing your ailing foot over hot burning steam for a considerable period of time in the hope of bringing about a cure? I have personally gone through that horrendous form of traditional medical practice!

Is it working hard to attain a goal only to face one obstacle after the other, amounting to a real threat of failure after years of effort? I have been there too.

Even as I write these lines, at a time when grey hair seems to have won the battle against the deep black hair for the right to occupy my head, I am not free from challenges.

I am not proclaiming my personal experience as the worst ever encountered by any human being. Indeed there have been, and there continue to be countless instances of heart-breaking stories of human suffering and misery. I am merely citing my own experiences of such suffering as one among millions.

So instead of resigning in the face of the seemingly unconquerable life challenges we are facing, let's get up, dust ourselves down and fight on!

9
DEALING WITH UNEXPECTED TWISTS AND TURNS

AT THE BEGINNING of September 1978, the GCE 'A'-Level results were released. I obtained the following Grades: biology B, physics D, chemistry E, general paper D (the general paper had little bearing on the university admission process).

Someone might have been excited at achieving the grades I attained. Not me! Without boasting, I knew I was capable of achieving something better. Indeed, I had reckoned with a minimum of three Bs in the three core subjects – amounting to an aggregate of six – which would have propelled me straight into one of the two medical schools in the country.

With an aggregate of eleven (B=2, D=4, E=5) my chance of being admitted to medical school was slim indeed. In the circumstances, it would have required me to have some connections at the top to gain admission to my cherished course of study. Indeed, as it turned out, some of my peers who obtained similar grades were admitted to medical school that year. They boasted of something I did not have – connections to people of influence in society.

Even so, I did entertain some hopes that I would be admitted. In those days, candidates applying for medicine and other well sought after courses such as law, pharmacy and business administration, were invited for pre-selection interviews.

In the case of less sought-after courses such as agricultural science, science, archaeology etc., the universities offered admission to successful applicants without interviews.

I waited and waited to be invited for a pre-selection interview to medical school – in vain. Eventually rumours reached me to the effect that the selection process to both medical faculties had ended and that some of the successful candidates had started receiving admission letters.

It was the practice in those days for each of the then three universities in the country to publish the list of students admitted to the first year in the two leading national dailies a few weeks prior to the beginning of the academic year. In the end my name appeared in the list of those admitted for a bachelor of science course.

A bachelor of science degree! It was a course of study for which I had zero interest and I was not prepared to allow anyone to force a course of study down my throat for which I had no interest whatsoever.

Though I recognised the need to be flexible in my career aspirations, I also realised the importance of not allowing the circumstances to force me into a course of study for which I had no interest.

Over the next several days, I was not only saddened at the turn of events but also confused – very confused indeed.

Being upset when we face disappointments is a natural reaction. The important thing, however, is that we do not resign ourselves to our fate. After the initial shock came my resolve to explore a possible way out of the situation.

I recognised two options:

a) I could pursue a different course of study.
b) I could re-sit the examination in an attempt to improve my grades.

In regard to pursuing a different course of study, the situation was not clear cut. While medicine was my primary interest, law and journalism were the two other fields of study I had some interest in.

The interest constellation, comprised of medicine, law and journalism, was however problematic. If it had been, for example, medicine, pharmacy and agricultural science, the migration from one to the other would have been easier due to the subject combination I offered at the sixth-form level.

To be considered for law and journalism one had to pass three arts subjects in the 'A'-Level examination. Having offered three science subjects to meet the criteria for medicine, I had all but excluded myself from the possibility of being considered for admission into those areas.

What about re-sitting the examination? That option was not feasible for several reasons.

While remedial courses were offered by private institutions, the course fees were beyond the means of my parents.

There was also no guarantee that I would be selected the following year if I managed to improve my grades. As I mentioned earlier on, competition for admission into the two medical schools was very strong. I would have had to compete with fresh 'A'-Level graduates passing out of sixth form that year for the few available places. My information was that, during the selection, preference was given to applicants who had passed out of sixth form in the particular year that the selection was taking place.

10
LET'S KEEP ON EXPLORING FEASIBLE ALTERNATIVES RATHER THAN GIVE UP!

IT WAS IN THE MIDST of the confusion regarding the future that I paid a visit to a friend in Accra. When he learnt of my situation, he not only consoled me, but opened my eyes to an alternative path that offered good prospects of helping me achieve my goal.

He was an executive member of the Ghana Soviet Friendship Society (GSFS), and told me that every year a considerable number of scholarships were granted to members to study in various universities and institutes of higher learning in the then Soviet Union. By virtue of being a member of the executive, he would take part in the selection process. He would make sure I was selected, he assured me.

The only thing I needed to do was to become a member. He therefore advised me to attend the next meeting that was due to take place in a few days' time and formally register as a member.

Perhaps at this stage I should explain briefly what was then referred to in Ghana as the Eastern Scholarship Scheme. It was a scheme whereby the countries of the then Eastern Bloc placed hundreds of scholarships at the disposal of students from the developing world – from Africa, South America and Asia – to study in the countries behind the so-called Iron Curtain. The scholarships were allegedly offered without any strings attached. At the back of the minds of the donors was of course the hope that the beneficiaries after their long stay in their society would return to propagate the communist ideology in their various countries.

In Ghana the bulk of the scholarships were channelled through the Scholarships Secretariat, a government agency. Up until my visit to my friend, I was not aware that members of the GSFS could also benefit from the scheme.

I joined the organisation as recommended. To prepare for a possible stay in the Soviet Union, members were encouraged to study the Russian language. For that purpose I registered for the free course at the Soviet Cultural Centre in Accra. Over the next several weeks, I attended the twice-weekly evening classes, each session lasting 90 minutes.

I was invited for an interview in the middle of January 1979. A little over a week later, the good news of my selection to study medicine in the Soviet Union reached me.

The sequence of events from selection to the departure to the Soviet Union were explained to the successful candidates as follows:

First the list of the selected beneficiaries would be sent to the Soviet Union where the beneficiaries would be assigned to universities and institutions of higher learning in various parts of the country.

Several weeks prior to the departure to the Soviet Union, the final list, showing beneficiaries and their assigned institutions, would be sent back to Ghana.

At that stage the beneficiaries would be issued the necessary travel documents including a free plane ticket. The final departure to the Soviet Union would be around the middle of August.

Apart from free tuition, boarding and lodging, we were told, we would also receive pocket money, not only from the Soviet authorities but from the Ghana government as well.

Words could hardly express my delight on the prospect of studying in the Soviet Union. For a while, I even considered it a blessing in disguise that I missed the chance to study in Ghana.

Just as I was rejoicing at the good news, the unexpected happened – my name was eliminated from the list even prior to being sent to the Soviet Union for the first time! The reason given was that an oversight had occurred in the selection process. Being a national organisation the scholarships were meant to benefit residents of the whole country. The Southern Branch of the organisation, I was told, had failed to consider candidates from the Northern Branch in the selection process. The mistake needed to be remedied. As a result, the original list had been revised, with the result that the names of a few successful candidates, including mine, had been eliminated from it.

As might be expected, I wanted to know why I had been eliminated. The reason I was given was that when I walked into the interview room, I appeared to be limping on my left leg. The executive members, some of whom had been in the Soviet Union themselves, considered that a disadvantage. They thought that whatever problem was behind my impairment would worsen when exposed to the severe winter conditions of the Soviet Union!

My left ankle – it had not only led to two long years of interruption in my primary education, but had also dashed my hopes of studying medicine in the Soviet Union!

As one might imagine, I was devastated by the unexpected turn of events.

To attend an interview, to be told a week later I had been selected, to share the good news with the whole world, to start preparing my mind for an impending trip oversees, only to be told at that advanced stage my name had been eliminated, was a really bitter disappointment. For the next several days, I was inconsolable.

It is a natural reaction to feel disappointed when things do not go your way. It is important however that we do not allow the circumstances to overwhelm us – to the point of giving up on our aspirations and throwing in the towel.

After a brief spell of heartache, I resolved not to give up my attempt to go to the Soviet Union that year – no, not until I had exhausted every possible avenue available to me.

I sat down to review the situation. It was towards the middle of February. Someone told me the list of the selected beneficiaries was usually dispatched to the Soviet Union sometime in March. As long as that had not yet happened it might be revised. What could I do to get my name re-instated?

Someone made me aware of the national president of the organisation. He happened to be the Navro Pio, I was told. To those unfamiliar with Ghana, the Navro Pio is a traditional leader of an ethnic group of an area in and around Navrongo, a large town in the north of the country. I was told that he had some influence with the Soviets, having studied there several years before. He could probably use his good connections with them to get them to create one or two additional scholarships for that year. My source went on to state that he had done so on some occasions in the past. I was therefore urged to speak to him personally on the matter.

Navrongo is situated about 850 kilometres to the north of Accra. A journey between the two cities meant literally crossing almost the whole of Ghana from north to south. Though my financial resources were scarce, I decided to sacrifice all to make the journey.

I might as well have spared myself the stress and the expenses involved in the undertaking. Though he was sympathetic, he made it clear to me that he was incapable of helping me.

Though I was disappointed, I took consolation in the fact that I had done my utmost best. If I had not taken that step, I would have been haunted by the thought that, had I done so, things might have taken a different turn. Having exhausted all possible avenues, I could console myself with the thought that I had at least done all that was humanly possible.

I believe we must strive to put in our humanly best and leave the rest to Providence. We cannot after all do more than our best, can we? We should, however, learn not to throw in the towel too early. Indeed, when we are knocked down, let's learn to get up and run; in fact, let's keep on running as long as we have breath in our bodies! As Winston Churchill once said in an address to a group of schoolchildren during the war: 'Never give in, never give in, never, never, never, never – in nothing, great or small, large or petty – never give in except to convictions of honour and good sense.'

11
WHEN MISFORTUNE STRIKES, LET'S AVOID ENGAGING IN ENDLESS SELF-PITYING

THE CHANCE TO STUDY at the Ghana Medical School had gone with the wind; the chance to study in the Soviet Union had been shattered – both events happening one after the other, indeed, barely six months apart, and it was really difficult to bear.

To say that I was not hugely disappointed would give the impression that I am super human. In fact, over the next several days, I was overwhelmed with grief. In such situations, we have the tendency to indulge in self-pity, even to engage ourselves in an exaggerated or self-indulgent pity, thinking of ourselves as the victim who has done no wrong and is deserving of condolence from everyone.

In my African culture, we have the tendency, in such situations, to assign blame to witchcraft and wizards, believing that members of our family, both nuclear and extended, have cast spells on us!

Did I, if only for a while, indulge in self-pity? Well, the events I am narrating took place several years ago, so I cannot exactly recall my feelings at that time. Even if I was tempted to succumb to self-indulgent pity, however, it was not for long.

It is indeed important that when faced with adversity, the most terrible misery imaginable, we do not resign ourselves to our fate. Instead, we should strive to look out for ways and means of escape.

Towards the end of August 1979, the group selected to study in the Soviet Union left the country, bringing to an end all my hopes of studying in the Soviet Union that year.

The illusory certainty of going to the Soviet Union that year had prevented me from concentrating on my studies or applying to be considered for admission into a different field of study. Facing an uncertain future after my Soviet dreams were dashed, I pondered on my next step. I realised I had two options:

1) Bury my cherished goal of studying medicine in the sand and pursue the course offered me or apply for a different course of study at one of the three universities in Ghana.
2) Steadfastly hang on to my original goal of studying medicine.

Concerning the first alternative, the situation was not clear-cut as far as the Bachelor of Science degree was concerned. I had missed many compulsory practical sessions, which meant I could face an uphill task convincing the department to permit me to make up for lost time.

For a while, I considered pursuing a degree in agricultural science. In that respect, too, the situation was not straightforward. It was September 1979. Having failed to apply for admission that year, the earliest I could be admitted – if at all – would be in the October of the following year.

In regard to holding on to my original goal of studying medicine, though the executive of the GSFS had indicated that I would be given priority in the selection process the following year, I refused to hang my hopes on their promise, especially in the light of the experience I had gone through. Rumours had in the meantime begun to circulate to the effect that money changed hands in the selection process. Someone hinted to me that if I had offered the executive 'something' I would probably have been allowed to travel. If that were the case, where then was the guarantee that my application would be successful the following year, since in any case I would not be in a position to offer 'something' on that occasion as well?

12
AGAIN AND AGAIN WE MAY HAVE TO START AFRESH!

AT THAT POINT IN MY LIFE I had a close associate, a member of our church. We were doing a good deal of things together. My associate's sister-in-law, a German citizen, was keen to help her join her in Germany. Preparations for her trip were in an advanced stage.

Having followed the twists and turns in my fortunes regarding my two futile attempts to get to medical school, she had developed some sympathy for me. One day, she turned to me:

'Well,' she said to me, 'I cannot give you a hundred percent assurance of help – but in case I manage to get to Germany, I will do whatever I can to help you come over to study there.'

I wondered, if I did not make it to medical school in Ghana and the Soviet Union, could I end up studying in Germany?

To underscore her determination to help settle her in Germany, the sister–in–law of my associate paid for her to attend a 'German for beginners' course at the Goethe Institute in Accra.

Perhaps, I thought to myself, I should enrol for the 'German for beginners' course as well. After all, 'Russia for beginners' had proved pointless – so perhaps 'German for beginners' would prove to be a better investment!

I put the thought into action and soon I was attending the 'German for beginners' classes at the premises of the Goethe Institute in Accra. It was a twice-weekly evening event with each session lasting 90 minutes.

I lived quite a distance from the Institute. That, coupled with lack of funds to pay for transportation, led to several abstentions on my part. At the end of the course, which as far as I can recall lasted six weeks, apart from learning the alphabet, a few words relating to greetings and the names of the days and months, I had learnt very little by way of the German language.

At the Goethe Institute I made enquiries concerning the entry requirements for foreign students intending to study in Germany. In the event I found out the following:

1) Tuition was free for every student at German universities, foreign students included.
2) An applicant from Ghana has to attain three passes at the GCE 'A-Level' and show proof of sufficient knowledge of the German language.
3) The candidate should provide evidence of being in a position to fund his or her education.
4) Candidates were encouraged to apply to the universities from their native countries and await their admission letters.
5) With an admission letter and proof of financial support they could apply for a student's visa at the German embassy. One had to provide satisfactory proof of being able to pay for his/her stay. That entailed, I was told, providing credible evidence of a monthly remittance of around 500 German marks from parents, a guardian or a recognisable organisation.

It has been said that someone looking at a bottle filled to the middle with water or fluid can either see it as half-full or half-empty. The born optimist that I am, I saw the bottle as half full!

Yes, I focused on the two requirements that favoured me – three passes at 'A'-Level as well as free tuition for all. While not completely neglecting the unfavourable factors, I just refused to dwell on them. From that moment I began to think and dream big – of studying medicine in Germany!

What point do we gain on dwelling on the negative? I have come across those who have such a pessimistic attitude to life and it just stuns me. Mortals as we are, we do not know whether what we have set out to do will succeed after all. A great many of the decisions we make in life could in the end be considered gambles. I choose to look at the brighter side of things and hope for the best rather than look at the darker side and be paralysed by the fear of failure.

13
LET'S NOT BECOME TIRED OF KNOCKING ON EVERY DOOR THAT OFFERS HOPE OF PROGRESS

IN FEBRUARY 1980, my acquaintance made it to Germany. Whilst keeping her promise to help me get there at the back of my mind, I decided to explore other possibilities of getting there by my own steam.

In the event it dawned on me that I had two options:

The first was to follow the advice provided by the Goethe Institute and apply directly to the various universities from Ghana and await an admission letter and with it apply to the German embassy for a student's visa. I considered that option a non-starter. How could I get my poor parents at Mpintimpi to issue the financial declaration needed for the student's visa?

The second alternative was to attempt to get to Germany by 'the back door'. How, one might ask, did the 'back door' route to Germany function? It existed because of the unique status of West Berlin during the time of the Cold War. As readers may recall, West Berlin was a kind of a 'capitalist island' surrounded by communist

East Germany. The traveller from Ghana – like others from various parts of the developing world who followed the same route to West Berlin – only needed to make it to East Berlin with an East German transit visa. From East Berlin, one could take a train to cross over to West Berlin.

My associate encouraged me to attempt this 'back door' option in her letters to me. The moment I managed to set my foot on the soils of West Germany, I could apply for political asylum. I would subsequently be granted temporary leave to stay, which could give me time to apply to the universities. Once I got a university to admit me, I could get the authorities to issue me with a student's visa – so I was told.

How could I reach East Berlin from Ghana? I learnt that there were 'connection men' around who could, for a fee, obtain for me an East Berlin transit visa. Not able to pay the 'connection fee', I decided to go to the East German embassy to apply on my own. Though the official I met was forthcoming, my application was turned down on the grounds that I was unable to show sufficient hard currency – US dollars – as proof that I was capable of supporting myself during my stay.

14
AS WE STRUGGLE TO MAKE IT, SOCIAL PRESSURE MAY MOUNT

A CCRA, DECEMBER 1980: More than two years after passing out of sixth form, my hope of studying medicine was all but shattered. I was still hanging around at the University of Ghana in Legon as an undergraduate bachelor of science student.

My distaste for the course of study had prevented me from attending lectures. To wile away my time and also to earn additional income to supplement the stipend I was receiving as a student, I had secured a job as a clerical assistant at the Post and Telecommunications office in Accra.

Meanwhile, pressure began mounting on me – from an unexpected source! My parents, though illiterate, were aware that once I passed out of sixth form the next stage on my academic journey would be a course of study at the university. Somehow, word had reached faraway Mpintimpi to the effect that instead of attending university, I was working.

'Why not concentrate on your studies instead of working?' my parents queried me through someone who had returned to Accra following a visit to the village. 'No worries, everything is under control', I assured them through someone returning from Accra to the village.

Not that I was unaware of the fact that I could not carry on playing the role of the 'student in limbo' indefinitely. Though I had, up until then not received any queries from the university, it was clear to me that it was only a matter of time before pressure began to mount from that direction. If nothing changed, I would soon lose my student status and be forced out of the free students' accommodation I was occupying!

The circumstances threatened to overwhelm me; still, I did not lose hope!

15
LET'S NOT HANG ALL OUR HOPES ON OTHERS

IN OUR JOURNEY towards the achievement of our goal, we need to rely, first and foremost, on our own effort and ability. We may require assistance from our parents, relatives and outsiders, but at the end of the day it is our individual effort that must be the top priority.

How many times have I, with the best of intentions, promised to help others, only to realise that I was incapable of honouring my promise. The reason did not lie in my unwillingness to help – unforeseen circumstance just cropped up to squeeze my resources and render me incapable of keeping my word. The other party may feel disappointed, even accuse me of being self-centred and caring only for myself. If only they had known the real reason for my inability to help!

Contrary to the expectations of my associate, as a visitor to Germany her road was not as smooth as she had anticipated. Not permitted to work, she was living from the meagre benefits being handed out by the state as well as the occasional support received from her relations – as I learnt when I received her letters. She had, however, not forgotten her promise, she assured me – whenever she was in a position so to do, she would help me to travel to Germany.

How could I expect her to keep her promise anytime soon when she herself was struggling to make ends meet in her new environment?

16
WE MAY HAVE TO TAKE A GAMBLE ON THE FUTURE

IT WAS AT A TIME of complete uncertainty about my future when I bumped into Yaw, an acquaintance of mine, on the streets of Accra. I had got to know him through George, a close friend of mine at Oda Secondary School.

As it turned out, both of us were harbouring similar plans for the future. He was desirous of studying architecture in the U.S. His elder brother, who was already resident there, had promised to send him funds for the ticket as well as the required proof of financial support to take to the U.S. embassy in Accra for a student's visa. He had waited almost a year on his brother to fulfil his promise – in vain. He had decided therefore to take matters into his own hands, he remarked.

'What do you mean by "taking matters into your own hands"?' I asked him.

'I'm on my way to Nigeria to work to earn my plane ticket to the U.S. instead of waiting on my brother', he replied.

'Where will you stay?' I inquired.

'On a construction site!' he replied.

'Construction site?'

'Yes, in a building under construction. It belongs to a Nigerian citizen who used to reside in our village. She has permitted several young men from my village to reside there temporarily.'

Yaw's friends were not the only Ghanaians who had gone to find greener pastures in Nigeria.

The economy of oil-rich Nigeria, profiting from the oil crisis of 1979, was booming. The favourable economic climate had rejuvenated the labour market. Several hands were needed to work on the countless building and construction projects going on throughout that large country.

The buoyant economy had also led the federal government to introduce free education for all. Several new schools had been established to cope with the increased number of pupils enrolling to go to school.

A huge demand for teachers had arisen as a result of that policy which could not be satisfied by local staff alone. Ghana and Nigeria, being former English colonies, had a similar educational structure. Teachers from Ghana were thus highly welcomed in Nigeria.

As a result of these factors, Nigeria had become a great attraction, not only for Ghanaians but also nationals from other countries in the West African sub-region.

I decided to travel with Yaw to Nigeria with the aim of working to earn the means to travel on to West Germany.

17
IF ONLY FOR A WHILE WE MAY HAVE TO KEEP OUR PLANS TO OURSELVES

APART FROM the student with whom I shared my hostel room at the university campus, and the person I was travelling with, I kept everyone – my parents included – in the dark concerning my journey to Nigeria.

How could I expect my parents, especially my mother, to give their approval to such a venture – especially when news had reached Ghana to the effect that Lagos was a very dangerous place, particularly at night – and we were expected to arrive there at nightfall! Under the circumstances, I decided to keep matters to myself instead of sharing my plans with them.

There may indeed come moments, decisive moments, on our journey towards our goal when we may have, even for a short period, to keep things to ourselves.

18
WE MAY BE FORCED TO SLEEP ROUGH AND ENGAGE IN DIRTY, BONE-BREAKING JOBS TO ACHIEVE OUR GOAL

IN OUR JOURNEY towards the achievement of our goal we may be forced, if only temporarily, to sleep rough and also engage in unsavoury work – mean, dirty, bone-breaking jobs we previously would never have imagined performing.

Indeed, we may set out with guaranteed financial support from parents, relatives, etc. But we live in an unpredictable world. Any unforeseen circumstance could indeed set in to bring us into difficulty. Instead of the assured finances we set out with, we could end up having to spend hours jobbing at a fast food restaurant, packing heavy items at a delivery depot, or doing various jobs as a factory hand to earn income to live on.

At the time I was passing out of sixth form, it never occurred to me that barely 18 months later, circumstances would force me to engage in bone-breaking jobs to survive at a slum settlement in faraway Lagos!

How to Beat the Odds to Your Goal

Not that I was not used to hard work. Throughout the time I was growing up at Mpintimpi, I helped my parents on our farm. Though with the onset of the problem of my left ankle, I had been exempted from doing activities that could adversely affect it, I still helped at home and on the farm to the best of my ability.

With no money at hand and no relative or friend to appeal to, I had no choice but to settle for whatever accommodation and work I could lay my hands on. As I mentioned earlier, we joined a group of individuals from Yaw's village residing in a building still under construction. Only the ground floor and the first storey of what was to be a four-storey building were halfway complete. There was no running water there. A dug well actually inside the house provided the inhabitants as well as the construction workers with water. The toilet facilities were not yet in place… a dug-in lavatory served us! The kitchen was not completed either. We made use of kerosene stoves to do our cooking. We slept in groups of about five in rooms that were yet to be fitted with doors.

Not only was the accommodation mean, I was forced to earn my living performing tough, back-breaking manual jobs at the construction sites.

The undeclared motto of residents of the colony was: each man for himself and God for us all. Indeed each resident was expected to earn his daily living. To use the problem of my left leg as an excuse to stay away from work would have been tantamount to starvation. Ailing leg or not, I had to do whatever was required of the assistant hired to work on a construction site on a particular day. These included the following:

- Carrying bags of cement, water, sand, gravel, etc., on our heads, from storehouses that could be considerable distances away, to the construction sites.

- Mixing sand, cement and gravel to provide sufficient mortar needed for the day's work.
- Carrying the prepared mortar on our heads to masons on various floors of the building under construction.

There were some evenings when after returning from work my weak left ankle began to ache so badly I thought I could not return to work the next day. Was it because I desperately needed the income to survive?

Well, somehow, I managed to get up everyday, Monday to Saturday (the construction sites rested on Sundays) to walk around looking for work. Indeed, never throughout the approximately eight weeks that I resided in the half-finished accommodation in Lagos did I stay out of work on the grounds of ill health. My perseverance paid off.

19
UNEXPECTED EVENTS MAY SET IN TO THREATEN OUR PROGRESS

MORTALS AS WE ARE, we have no control over tomorrow. We should always therefore reckon with the unexpected – with events and occurrences man-made as well as natural that might set in to disrupt our progress, even to threaten or jeopardise our plans.

After spending about eight weeks at the 'construction site' in Lagos, I gained employment as a secondary school teacher at Shagamu, a large town about 80 kilometres to the north-east of Lagos. I took up my appointment in the middle of January 1981. Based on my earnings, I gave myself a maximum of a year to earn enough money to finance my journey to East Berlin.

In the middle of December 1981, at the time when I had saved about 70% of the money needed for my journey to Germany, the news of the sudden passing away of my senior brother, the first child of my parents, aged 38years, reached me.

If it had happened at a time when I had already booked my flight, at a time when my journey to Germany was imminent, I would have excused myself from the funeral.

As I mentioned earlier, I kept my family in the dark about my plans when I journeyed to Nigeria. In the course of time I informed them about my whereabouts.

There were also other residents of Amantia, mother's hometown, where the funeral was to take place, living in the very town where I was. The funeral was set for the time between Christmas and New Year. Even before the news reached us in Shagamu, several of the residents had expressed the desire to travel home for the Christmas period.

If I decided against attending the funeral so as not to jeopardise my plans to travel to Germany, how would family members – none of whom were aware of my wider future plans – react, especially when they learnt from those returning home for the Christmas holidays that I was in good health when they last saw me?

Partly as a result of these considerations, and especially due to a heartfelt desire to pay a personal farewell to my departed brother, I returned to Ghana a few days prior to Christmas 1981. My plan was to return to my post at the beginning of January 1982 and leave for Germany at the latest by June that year.

After the funeral ceremony, I made plans to return to Nigeria. Then came December 31, 1981!! The military seized power in Ghana and closed all borders – land, sea and air. Worse still, they issued a decree that required everyone leaving the country to first obtain an exit permit – which could be obtained only at a single location in the whole country, the Accra Sports Stadium.

As it turned out, a multitude of Ghanaians resident in Nigeria had flocked back to Ghana for the Christmas holidays with plans to return to their places of work in the first week of January. Everyone was keen to leave the country as soon as possible.

I left home very early on the first working day of January 1982 to apply for the exit permit, only to be met by huge crowds that had massed at the various gates of the national sports stadium in Accra.

I stood in the scorching sun for hours on the first day, only to return home empty-handed! I met the same fate on the second and third day! I was becoming desperate. Schools were re-opening in a matter of days in Nigeria. The agenda of the coup plotters was posing a real threat to my plans!!

On the fourth day, rumours began to circulate in Accra to the effect that the border guards at the border town Aflao, about 100 kilometres to the east of Accra, the crossing point I would need to pass on my return to Nigeria, were extorting money from travellers without permits in return for 'free' passage.

Well, I decided to take action – to go and find out.

If I had waited in Accra, I would have suffered the same fate as some of the teachers who obtained their permits weeks after the exercise began. They returned to their respective schools only to learn of the termination of their appointments.

On reaching Aflao, I experienced the confirmation of the rumours at first hand. Indeed, while the military junta that had seized power was busily rounding up former members of the previous government and high ranking public officials en mass and placing them behind bars, their fellow soldiers manning the borders were exhorting money from would-be travellers, lining their pockets by allowing them through at a price!

20
PROCRASTINATION IS THE THIEF OF TIME

IN LIFE, circumstances may, from time to time, force us to wait before taking the next step. It is, however, important that we refrain from waiting too long – beyond what is acceptable based on the circumstances. It is important that we do not postpone till tomorrow what we are capable of doing today.

As I mentioned earlier, I considered my stay in Nigeria a stepping stone towards my journey to Germany. Throughout my stay, which for me was temporary in order to fulfil a purpose, I regarded myself like a traveller sitting on parked luggage.

I had originally reckoned with leaving the country in January 1982. The events the reader is already aware of had forced me to spend some of my savings. Still, I wanted to leave as soon as possible.

I spoke to George, a good friend of mine. We had been friends since our days at Oda Secondary School. From Oda Secondary School, he went on to do a post-secondary education diploma in teaching. He had also joined the exodus of Ghanaians to Nigeria. At that time he was employed as a French teacher in Lagos.

I approached him for a loan to top up my savings. Bless him – he responded favourably.

Scarcely a year after my departure from Nigeria, the order came for the Ghanaians living there without residence permits to leave the country at short notice. Between half a million and a million people were affected. Although teachers were not directly affected by the deportation order, many of them, including almost all the Ghanaian staff at my former school, decided to leave voluntarily for their own safety. The attitude of the population to foreigners in general, and Ghanaians in particular, had turned hostile (they accused those groups of people not only of taking away their jobs but also of increased crime).

21
WE MAY NEED TO TAKE A PLUNGE INTO THE DEEP UNKNOWN!!

A TIME MAY COME on our journey to our goal when there may be the need to take a gamble; we may even have to undertake a risky action – a deep plunge into the unknown with an uncertain outcome.

My journey from Ghana to Nigeria on December 1, 1980 was not without risks. Neither Yaw nor me had ever been to Nigeria. Yet we knew at least that if we asked our way several times, we could finally find the location of the place. Besides that, as it was a member of the ECOWAS group of countries, we did not need a visa to reside in Nigeria, at least not during the first several weeks.

The situation was completely different when I embarked on my adventure to Europe on the night of May 11, 1982, armed only with an East Berlin visa I had obtained from the East German embassy in Lagos.

Not only did I face the real threat of immediate deportation (some who had gone before me had been arrested and sent back on the next available flight); I did not know for certain where I would spend my first night!

Still, I was determined to take the plunge into the deep unknown. It was not the quest for riches, fame, or privilege that drove me on. Rather, it was my desire to realise the goal of studying medicine that was prominent in my mind.

22
SOME SEEMING MISFORTUNES MAY TURN OUT TO BE BLESSINGS IN DIGUISE

WE ARE MERE MORTALS; we are not prophets endowed with the ability to foretell the future. We may encounter several twists and turns on our journey towards the attainment of our goals. Instead of moaning about our present misfortune, we should fight on and do our utmost, even in the present bad situation we may find ourselves in – for the adversity we are grumbling about today may well in the end turn out to be a blessing in disguise.

As I boarded the Balkan Airlines flight at the Lagos International Airport on my way to East Berlin, the following was my plan:

After emerging from the airport, I would board a train for a border checkpoint between East and West Berlin. From there I would take an underground train and head for West Berlin. That very night, or at the latest the next day, I would travel on from West Berlin to Hamburg to join the family of my acquaintance – the close associate I have already referred to. With their initial assistance, I hoped to find my way in the strange country and put my plans aimed at admission to medical school into action.

Things did not go the way I had envisaged though. In the end, I had to abandon my plans to move to Hamburg. Instead I had to remain in West Berlin.

In Hamburg I would have had a familiar face to turn to in the initial stages of my stay in the strange environment. In West Berlin, I had *zero contacts*. I was completely lost – lost, lost!

I was bitterly disappointed about the turn of events. However, it wouldn't take long for me to realise that being forced to stay in West Berlin was, after all, a blessing in disguise.

Indeed, if I had moved on to Hamburg as planned, I doubt very much that I would have realised my dream of studying medicine.

In Hamburg, I would, like my hosts, have been assimilated into the sizeable Ghanaian community living there at that time.

The first Sunday of my stay, I would have joined them to worship in their Church – a congregation that consisted almost completely of fellow asylum seekers. With the majority of them speaking English and Twi, the main Ghanaian local language, how would that have benefitted me – someone wishing to master the German language as soon as possible?

As asylum seekers, they were all subjected to the restrictions on work and free movement imposed on that group of individuals. With each of them literally struggling in their shoes, how could any of them have provided me meaningful assistance to realise my goal?

On my own in Berlin, with no familiar face to turn to, I had to fend for myself!

As an asylum seeker, I would have the right of free accommodation and also food.

The first thing I did, after being assigned a place in a hostel, was to look out for a church to worship in. Eventually, I found the American Lutheran Church in Berlin.

Joining that church turned out to be invaluable. Among other things, it led me to a German family that worshipped there. My association with them helped in my attempt to learn the German language, especially spoken German.

My association with the American Church in Berlin brought me into contact with Kurt, the German Pastor of the Paulus Gemeinde, a sister church of the American Church in Berlin. My contact with Kurt proved vital at the time I was applying to the university. He issued a letter of financial declaration to the effect that my living expenses would be taken care of in case I was admitted – a prerequisite for admission. He was also true to his word, for when I was admitted he provided financial support as promised.

The chain of favours resulting from my association with the American Church in Berlin would not end there. When I moved from West Berlin to begin my studies in Hanover, Kurt introduced me to Fredo, a friend of his who was resident there, who happened also to be a pastor. Eventually, Fredo's church offered me financial assistance.

Fredo also introduced me to Gottfried, the Superintendent Pastor responsible for several churches in the area of Hanover where I settled initially. My association with Gottfried and his family brought with it several advantages. Not only did I receive financial assistance from his church, Gottfried and his family opened the doors of their home to me. In the end I became almost like a member of their family.

During my stay in Berlin, I also got to know several German citizens – Ilse, Ruth, Rhea, Anna, etc., all of whom contributed to make my life in the strange environment bearable.

Have we on our life's journey been forced to make an unexpected halt in *West Berlin* instead of moving on to *Hamburg* as originally planned? Are we bitterly disappointed and upset by the turn of events?

Well, instead of grumbling over our fate, let's accept the situation and look out for the opportunities, for our 'angels', for those who might help turn our situation around.

23
WE MAY NEED TO LEARN NEW SKILLS ALONG THE WAY

I DID NOT have the opportunity to learn to ride a bike as a child. On my arrival in West Berlin, it soon dawned on me that I couldn't afford travelling on the tube train for long. The fares they demanded, while not being substantial for an average worker, were a lot for a person like me, given my scarce resources.

Besides the monetary consideration, there was another reason why I was not keen on using the underground as my main means of transportation. I wanted to be conversant with the city. Using the underground for the most part would only be a hindrance to achieving that goal.

On the other hand I realised the city boasted excellent cycle pathways. I thought of the bicycle as a good practical means of achieving the objectives outlined above.

I had a handicap though – I did not know how to ride a bike! Growing up under the impoverished conditions of Mpintimpi, I had not had the opportunity to learn to ride.

I decided to overcome that hurdle. In the end, I got one of the Ghanaian residents of the asylum hostel, who had that ability, to help me acquire the skill.

With the help of a second-hand bike I acquired for almost nothing from a flea market in the neighbourhood of the asylum hostel I went with my 'riding instructor' to a nearby park to begin my riding lessons.

After falling several times and sustaining bruises here and there, I finally succeeded in balancing myself on the device and managed to move a few metres without falling! Rarely did I travel on public transport thereafter.

My ability to ride a bike became an asset in the pursuit of my goal, enabling me to interact freely with those who mattered for me in Berlin. When at long last I initiated my studies at Hanover, it not only facilitated my movement, but also helped me save money that I would otherwise have spent on transportation.

24
EVEN IN SEEMINGLY DEAD-END SITUATIONS – LET'S PERSEVERE STILL!

EVEN IN SEEMINGLY dead-end situations on our journey to the fulfilment of our goal, we don't have to throw in the towel. 'Never say die until the bones are rotten!' – so the motto goes of Accra Hearts of Oak, one of the leading football clubs in Ghana.

So long as we have breath, we should never give up hope, however hopeless the situation may seem. Instead we need to look out for avenues to help turn things around. I was confronted with a similar situation shortly after my arrival in West Berlin.

Prior to my departure from Africa, I had been made to understand that, in order to be allowed to stay on in Germany, I would have to apply for political asylum. I was informed that the right of political asylum was enshrined in the German constitution. Since at that time Ghana was under a military dictatorship, that fact alone was enough for the authorities to grant me leave to stay.

What I was not told were the conditions under which the temporary leave to stay was granted. That would soon become clear to me.

After I had handed in my application, the first surprise came when I was asked to surrender my passport. 'When would it be returned to me?' I inquired. Not until a final decision had been made on my application, was the reply. Instead of my passport, I was handed a folded piece of paper bearing my picture.

'What is this for?' I asked the officer who handed it to me.

'It is your visa; you must keep it on you always so you can show it to any state authority checking on your residential status', was the reply.

Since it was in German I did not, at first, understand the details it contained. In the end I got a Ghanaian student I came across to interpret it for me.

Below is what I learnt:

It was a temporary visa, issued initially for six months. I was granted temporary leave of stay on the following grounds:

1) I was not permitted to take up employment or learn a trade.
2) Until my asylum case had been decided upon, I was not permitted to travel away from the federal state in which I was resident, in this case West Berlin.

When I let my countryman know the reason for my trip to Germany, he stated that each federal state treated asylum seekers posted there differently. As far as employment was concerned the matter was straightforward – no asylum seeker was permitted to work anywhere in the federation. In the case of embarking on studies, the provision was interpreted differently by the state authorities. Whereas some permitted asylum seekers to study the moment they gained admission, others did not. West Berlin, he went on to say, was one of the federal states that did not permit asylum seekers to study. Since I was resident there, the same would apply to me.

To compound my woe I was told that even if I gained admission to a university in a different federal state, the West Berlin authorities would not release my passport to enable me to embark on my studies.

All the named restrictions, I was told, would be lifted the moment my asylum application was granted.

What were the chances of an asylum application from Ghana being recognised, I wanted to know. Not good, was his reply. His information was that fewer than 1% of such applications were successful.

I had laboured all those months beforehand to make it to Germany to realise my cherished goal only to realise that I would not be permitted to study after all! *I was indeed trapped in Berlin!!*

Under the circumstances, I had two options:

1) Resign myself to my fate, do nothing and await my certain deportation in a matter of months. (I was told that asylum applications of Ghanaians took about a year to go through all the legal processes.)
2) Continue to pursue my goal of making it to medical school in defiance of the seemingly hopeless situation.

25
'I DID NOT TRAVEL ALL THE DISTANCE FROM MPINTIMPI TO BERLIN TO GIVE UP!'

LIFE IS A MARATHON, not a sprint. A sprint is finished in a matter of seconds whereas a marathon will last for a matter of hours. A 100-metre race is run on a flat level track, whereas it is very rare to find a marathon race that is run entirely along a flat and even terrain. The likelihood is that it will be run along different types of landscapes: plains, hills, hillocks – in short, over ups and downs.

In as much as a marathon is hardly run on a plain even track, it is very likely that the path we will tread in our journey towards our goal will be rough and uneven. How we deal with the hurdles, obstacles and seemingly impossible situations is what makes the difference between success and failure.

I read about the feat of the late John Stephen Akhwari, a marathon runner who ran for his country, Tanzania, in the 1968 Mexico City Olympic Games. It was the last event of the games. Early in the race he suffered a bad fall and, in the process, badly injured his leg. Though he trailed a considerable distance behind the others, he kept running instead of giving up. In the end he finished the race nearly an hour behind the rest of the runners.

How to Beat the Odds to Your Goal

When Akhwari finally approached the stadium, running on his badly injured and hurting leg, it was nearly empty. As he entered the stadium the meagre crowd still present rose to their feet and began to cheer. Photographers scrambled to set up the cameras they had long since dismantled to capture what without doubt would be regarded as one of the greatest finishes in Olympics history. Later, when asked why he did not quit, Akhwari said simply:

'My country did not send me 5,000 miles to start the race; they sent me 5,000 miles to finish the race!'

Indeed, the path to the attainment of our goal will not be without challenges – minor and major. The question that we will have to ponder when we stand before the seemingly insurmountable hurdles is: did we embark on the journey, or set off on the race, just for the sake of participation – or did we indeed set out to finish it, come what may!?

Though the situation I faced appeared hopeless, I vowed to do whatever was within my means to change it.

I did not set out from Ghana, go through the experience the reader is familiar with in Nigeria, travel on to East Berlin and cross over to West Berlin, only to end up in an asylum hostel, condemned to a life of boredom and inactivity, with certain deportation back to Africa looming on the horizon.

As a first step I travelled to the Free University, one of the two universities in West Berlin at that time, to find out at first hand their admission requirements. One might wonder why I took that step since I had already received the information at the Goethe Institute in Accra. The answer is that I wanted to obtain the information from the 'horse's own mouth'.

My visit to the foreign students' secretariat of the said university was worth the effort, as it turned out. Apart from getting confirmation of what I already knew, one clearer detail emerged. Prior to this I was aware that I needed to show sufficient proof of knowledge of the German language. What 'sufficient proof of knowledge' entailed became clear to me on my visit. As an applicant from Ghana, I was told, I needed to present a GCE 'O'-Level pass with a minimum of Grade 'C'!

26
WE MAY NEED TO TEACH OURSELVES LATIN TO PROGRESS!

HOW COULD I MANAGE to present a pass at GCE 'O'-Level – not with Grade 'D' nor Grade 'E', but Grade 'C' or above in the shortest possible time?

Not aware of my financial situation, the official, a friendly lady in her middle forties, pointed me to the International Translators Institute in the city. One could not only register for an intensive course there, she said, but could also take the GCE 'O'-Level test there.

I thanked the official for the information and made for the ITI in Berlin – not with the aim of registering for an intensive German language course but to find out when the next GCE 'O'-Level test was due.

In the end, I found out that the earliest opportunity to take the test was in November that year. The registration fee was around two hundred US dollars. The deadline for registration was within a matter of weeks. It was towards the end of May. If I were to take the test that year, I needed to hurry up!

Entertaining the faint hope of making it to Germany had led me to spend a few weeks at the Goethe Institute in Accra. As I mentioned earlier, apart from becoming familiar with the alphabet and a few German phrases, my time there did not significantly advance my proficiency in the language itself. Two years on, having of late been exposed to Yoruba (one of the main languages spoken in Nigeria) and English – proper English as well as Pidgin English as spoken in Nigeria – almost nothing was left of my German.

I sat down to ponder the situation. Though, as already stated, my visa did not allow me to work or learn an apprenticeship, it did not bar me from studying the German language.

The quickest way of learning the language was by way of the intensive course as suggested by the university. For reasons already familiar to the reader, that path was a non-starter.

The second avenue, though not as promising as the first, was by way of the *Volkshochschule* (Worker's College). They usually operated in the evenings and offered various courses to the general public. Though their fees were subsidised, I could not afford them. In the end the only option left for me was *to teach myself* the language.

Having made up my mind, I set out looking for a suitable textbook to help me realise my goal. After spending time visiting one bookshop after the other, I eventually came upon a book titled *German for Beginners*.

Even today, I still wonder if the author had me, and me alone, in mind when he set out to write it. It was indeed a book that met my aspirations head on! A 'teach-yourself' book, it was intended for people with a command of the English language desiring to study the German language on their own. Every line in German, be it part of a passage, be it an example in sentence construction, be it lessons in the correct use of words, carried a colloquial or idiomatic English translation immediately beneath it.

And so, armed with my copy of *German for Beginners*, I set out to teach myself German. Working through it was such a pleasure – the moment I got hold of it I never wanted to part with it.

27
A HOSTILE ENVIRONMENT IS NO EXCUSE TO GIVE UP TRYING!

MY FIRST OFFICIAL ADDRESS in West Berlin was in the street bearing the name Schoeneberger Ufer, in a suburb known as Schoeneberg. It was a hostel operated by the German Red Cross. It was a six-storey building complex.

It was a men's only hostel and provided accommodation for several dozen asylum seekers from various parts of the developing world – from Pakistan to Afghanistan through to Lebanon and right down to Ghana. One could well describe it as a mini-United Nations of the developing world.

I was assigned to a room on the sixth floor, room 601. I shared it with three other asylum seekers from Ghana. One of the inmates had a very good sense of humour. That, combined with the fact that our room happened to be adjacent to the staircase, helped to turn it into a kind of meeting point for other Ghanaians living in the hostel, in particular those sharing the floor with us.

Not the best of environments for someone keen on teaching himself the German language. In time it became increasingly difficult for me to concentrate to work there. Fortunately the hostel happened to be located near a large public library. So, whenever the atmosphere in room 601 became unsuitable for academic work, I put on my clothes, placed my *German for Beginners* in a polythene bag and left the noisome room for the library.

The discovery of the library brought me an important advantage. I made use of some of the leading national and international dailies as well as magazines supplied to the library to improve my skills in the language I sought to master. My strategy was the following: first I went through a story making the headline in English. Next, I tried to understand the story in German.

28
LET'S NOT BE BOTHERED BY WHAT OTHERS SAY OR THINK ABOUT OUR PLANS

IF WE EXPECT everyone around us to speak words of encouragement to urge us on towards the attainment of our goal, we will wait in vain. We live in an imperfect world, inhabited by imperfect individuals. Some out of envy may say or act to dissuade us from achieving our goal. Others, for reasons best known to themselves, may do likewise.

In our little village, everyone knew one another. When Ransford, the second oldest child of my parents, passed the common entrance examination, my parents, despite our precarious financial situation, decided to pay for his education.

Father used to tell us that during that time not a few of the inhabitants tried to dissuade him from his undertaking.

'Why spend all your income on one child, when you have several others?' remarked one resident.

'Why keep on taking loans to pay for the boarding fees of one single child!' added another.

Determined to do what he deemed right, my father remained unmoved.

His efforts were rewarded – without doubt his offspring are among those who prospered the most in the village.

Several years later he was personally rewarded when one of his children, resident in Germany, invited him to visit that country. One can imagine how someone who had grown up in our deprived environment felt on his trip to Germany. In the meantime, nothing had changed in the living conditions of those who tried to dissuade him from offering his children the chance of higher education.

Not only were my roommates at Blumenhof noisy, they did not cease from trying to dissuade me from my effort, making the following points:

'Why waste your time learning such a difficult language?' one of them remarked.

'Why waste your time studying the language of these wicked people [the Germans]?' the other added.

'We came to Europe to earn money. The priority is to look for work to help us achieve our goal', said another, as if on behalf of the rest.

Several years later, after I had taken up my studies in Hanover, I returned to Berlin to do my electives at the surgery of a Ghanaian doctor resident there.

In the course of my four-week duty in the surgery, one of my former cohorts turned up for treatment. He was stunned to discover what had become of me. At the time of our meeting his asylum case was still pending – he was still not allowed to work or travel outside Berlin!

29
EXPECT UNEXPECTED OPPOSITION

WE LIVE IN A WORLD not devoid of jealousy, envy, backbiting, mistrust, bitterness, etc. Not everyone will wish us well, will want us to prosper. Just because we want to get on well with everyone; just because we do not want to bear anyone any grudge, just because we do not want to offend anyone, does not mean everyone will reciprocate our gestures or appreciate our motives.

I was determined to take the GCE 'O'-Level exam in November in order to fulfil one of the key requirements for university admission. An important hurdle needed to be overcome though – the registration fee. Needless to mention, here, it was far beyond my means.

When I mentioned the matter to Emmanuel and Tony, two Ghanaian students I had in the meantime got to know, they pointed me in the direction of the Ghana Students' Union in Berlin. I was told that, besides membership fees, they used to organise concerts, cultural events and other social events with the goal of raising funds for the organisation. Part of the money, I was told, had been set aside as a social fund to offer financial assistance by way of short-term loans to members in financial need.

My two acquaintances gave me the contact number of the general secretary and advised me to call him to discuss the matter. He was forthcoming on the phone, confirming that they had enough funds to meet my needs. He could however not decide on the matter alone. He urged me therefore to attend their general meeting which was about two weeks away and present my case to the whole assembly.

I did as he advised. Towards the end of the meeting, I was given the chance to present my case to the gathering. After giving a brief background about myself and why I was in Berlin, I mentioned the main reason why I was requesting their assistance.

When I was done, the president of the organisation got up to speak, in the process urging the members to give me the chance by unanimously supporting my request.

Next, he gave members the opportunity to air their views on the matter. Speaker after speaker followed and the idea of granting me the loan received support from the plenum.

Just when I thought the issue had received unanimous support from the plenum, one of the leading members of the organisation got up to speak.

'I am not against the principle of helping our countrymen and countrywomen who find themselves in difficulty', he began. 'In this particular instance, however, I want to appeal to members to reconsider their decision to grant our fellow member a loan.'

'Why?' the chairman inquired, surprised.

'I will cite three reasons to support my case', he continued. 'In the first place, I am only prepared to invest money in someone when I am convinced my investment has the chance of yielding results. Now we are all aware that the authorities these days strictly forbid asylum seekers from working or studying. In the second place, how can we be sure that our friend will be able to pass the test? Finally, where is the guarantee that he will be able to make the repayment?'

Happily, the majority did not share his misgivings and voted in favour of the loan.

Even as I write today, I ask myself: What was his motive?

Why didn't he, like the rest of the group, want to give me the chance? Why did he choose to dwell on the negative instead of the positive?

We should indeed be prepared for those who, for reasons best known to themselves, will seek to place obstacles, stumbling blocks, impediments, hurdles and what have you in our way to prevent us from attaining our goal.

30
EVEN IN THE FACE OF ADVERSITY LET'S REMAIN FOCUSSED!

HAVING PASSED the German language test in November 1982, happily with Grade 'C', my plan was then to apply for university admission without delay.

Then, as now, most German universities admit students twice annually – to the summer semester beginning April 1 and the winter semester starting October 1.

Those applying to be considered for admission to the summer semester have up to January 15 to submit their application. Those applying for the winter semester need to submit their application by July 15.

The results of my German test as well as some supporting documents I had requested from Ghana arrived too late for me to meet the January 15 deadline. My plan, therefore, was to apply for the winter semester of 1983. My information was that German applicants had to channel their application through an agency handling applications from the whole federation.

Foreign students, on the other hand, could apply directly to the university of their choice. There was no restriction on the number of universities one could apply to. My information was that each university reserved a certain percentage of their vacancies for foreign applicants.

Just as I was making plans to apply to the universities, the problem of my left ankle – readers may recall that the same problem was cited as the main reason for my exclusion from the Soviet scholarship scheme – resurfaced with a vengeance! Not only did it begin to swell up, but the pain became unbearable – to the extent that I could hardly bear to put any weight on it.

Towards the end of December 1982, the condition had deteriorated to the extent that the doctors advised surgery as the only cure.

'What on earth is behind it?' I asked the consultant handling it.

'It's my guess you've lived with it for some time?' he inquired.

'Yes, indeed, more than 15 years!' I replied.

'That comes as no surprise to me', he said. 'As it is, part of the bone forming the ankle is dead!'

'So I am a dead man walking!' I exclaimed.

'Well, I did not say that!' he smiled. 'In any case we want to help you. It's going to be quite a complicated surgery. We shall cut away those parts of the bone that have died and rebuild the joint. The procedure will leave the joint stiff, but I expect a good outcome.'

'How long will I stay in hospital?'

'Several weeks, if not months!' was the reply.

The surgery was finally performed in February 1983. My discharge from hospital was open ended – the doctors mentioned sometime in May or June. What was to be done in regard to my university application?

The application process at that time first required me to write to the various universities stating my qualifications and requesting admission forms. After about two weeks, those universities wishing to consider the application despatched a form comprised of several pages that the applicant needed to fill in and return with the appropriate supporting documents. How could I achieve that from my hospital bed?

I discussed the matter with Tony on one of his visits.

'No problem', he smiled, 'you can use my address. I will do my best to visit you every Saturday. I will bring with me any mail that may have arrived in the course of the week.'

In the course of time the forms began to pile up on the small mobile writing desk at my disposal in my hospital room. Without delay, I set about filling in the forms.

I needed to overcome another hurdle before I could submit the completed admission forms – I needed to affix a recent passport-sized photograph on them. I did not have any – and neither was there any automatic machine in the premises of the hospital where I could get them done.

When I spoke to Emmanuel on the matter he offered to help me out of the situation. In the end, with the permission of the doctors, he fetched me with a wheelchair and pushed me along the pavement bordering on a major road to a photo shop about two kilometres away to get the photographs taken.

31
LET'S NOT SETTLE FOR MEDIOCRITY!!

AT THE TIME I was filling in the forms, I was told that my chances of being admitted into medicine were almost nil. I was therefore advised to opt for a less competitive course, for example general science. Once I gained admission, I could, in the course of time, apply for admission into a medical degree programme.

Readers might recall that I had turned down a similar science degree course in Ghana. Because Ghana boasted only a few universities, the chance of one being able to switch from a degree course in science to medicine was almost nil. The situation was different in Germany, I was told. Due to the large number of universities, students had more flexibility in their choices of study.

After pondering the matter for a while, I decided to persevere in my choice for my ultimate goal. I had not turned down the subject I had no interest for in Ghana only to travel the distance to Germany to study the same course. At least on my first attempt, I would go for the absolute prize. I would only consider going for something less challenging if I was not successful on my first attempt to enter a medical programme of study.

In all, I applied to about a dozen universities spread throughout the federation – Berlin, Hamburg, Dusseldorf, Hanover, etc. In each case I chose medicine as my first choice.

Towards the end of June 1983 I was released from hospital. Though I still needed a pair of crutches to mobilise myself, I was confident I would be able to take up my studies in case I was admitted.

I was told to expect the outcome of my applications anytime from the beginning of August. That was indeed the case. Starting from that period, letters from the various universities began to pour in. I checked regularly with Tony, whose address I had used. I would open the letters, only to learn, one after the other, that my application had been rejected.

One day, after I had received no less than ten rejection letters, I received a letter from the Hanover Medical School offering me admission!

Why was I successful with Hanover but not with the rest?

Several years later, in a conversation with the secretary responsible for the affairs of foreign students, I learnt that at the time I applied for admission, the medical school had, for a while, been looking to admit someone from the West African sub-region. They had a system in place that aimed at allocating the admissions reserved for students from developing countries fairly among the various geographical regions concerned, I was told. For a while they had not received any suitable application from the West African sub-region.

From this I can distil the following important lesson: as we journey on to our goal in life, we should not allow the odds, however formidable, from discouraging us from putting in the necessary efforts towards the realisation of our objective.

Even if the chances of being accepted for the position we are aspiring to are slim, so long as we fulfil the basic requirements, the perceived odds should not necessarily serve as a deterrent. How can we tell from the outset if a quality, a character trait, a skill, even something unique to our application, might in the end prove to be the deciding factor that will carry the day in our quest?

32
IF NEEDS BE, LET'S TAKE OUR CASE TO THE OBAMAS OF OUR TIME!

———◆◇◆———

AS I MENTIONED before, contrary to expectations, I was admitted to the Hanover Medical School for the winter semester 1983–1984. The plan was for me to take a German language test at the university in the last week of September and matriculate on October 1.

Words can hardly describe my joy when I opened the large envelope enclosing not only the admission letter but also further information for first-year students. Soon I pictured me in my mind's eye, mingling with about half a dozen other students, following on the trail of a consultant on ward rounds, just the way it used to happen on a weekly basis in the hospital where I was admitted.

My joy was short-lived though. Indeed, on yet another occasion on my tortuous life journey so far, my ship of hope would hit the rocks!

I mentioned earlier in my narration that, when I applied for asylum, my passport was taken away from me. I had in the meanwhile learnt from various sources of several instances where asylum seekers had been allowed to take up their studies the moment they got a university to offer them admission.

With that in mind, I approached the responsible authorities in Berlin to request the return of my passport. The reply was negative – as long as my asylum application had not been granted, my passport would not be handed back.

Politics, bureaucracy, legalities of our time! That is the world we live in. We may indeed hit not one, not two but several bureaucratic hurdles on our way to our goal. I do not have any firm answers here. One has to deal with them based on the unique situation.

In my case, I decided to appeal to the Mayor of West Berlin for help. My strategy was the following: whilst aware of the need to uphold the law, I wanted him to grant me an exemption on humanitarian grounds – on the basis of the impairment in my left leg.

If his facial expression was anything to go by, the Mayor was clearly moved by my situation. In the end he delegated matters to his secretary who was present at the meeting, asking me to see him later to sort the matter out for me.

When I met his subordinate three days later, he lashed out at me, accusing me – wrongly of course – of trying to rob his daughter of the right to study medicine.

Though my effort did not bring the expected results, the thought that I had exhausted all avenues available to me at that time put my mind at rest.

Years later, when I published a book detailing the account of my path to medical school, I sent him a copy of the German translation. Several weeks later he wrote back, expressing delight that despite the hurdles I went through, I managed in the end to attain my goal.

We have to be bold and fearless on our life's journey. If we need to bring our case before the highest authority on earth, yes, even if it means before the Obamas of our time, so be it!

At the end of the day such individuals are just as human as we are. They are subjected to the problems and burdens that plague you and me. In the area of health, they are not spared headaches, backaches, stomach ache, toothache, and all the aches that we are subjected to by virtue of our common humanity.

On the emotional level, they are also subjected to all the negative feelings that are the lot of humanity – fear, anger, sadness, disgust, etc. What singles them out from us is the high office they are occupying. So if we think we have a genuine case that needs to be brought to the attention of the highest authority capable of helping to address it, we should not hesitate to do so.

33
LET'S NOT ALLOW THE FAILURES OF OTHERS TO DISCOURAGE US

LET US HOLD ON tenaciously to our plans. So long as we are convinced about what we are doing, we should move forward. We should not allow the misfortunes of those engaged in the same or a similar venture to discourage us. The fact that they have failed to make it in an undertaking similar to ours does not necessarily imply that the same destiny awaits us.

In August 1984, I was offered a second chance to study at the Hanover medical School.

Before I could formally be enrolled as a student, I needed to pass a German language test organised by the Hanover University for all foreign students wishing to study at that university as well as other institutions of higher learning in the city – the medical school included.

The test was decisive – though I had been offered admission, I could not engage in my studies without passing the test.

The test consisted of three parts – grammar, what was known in German as *Textwiedergabe* (reproducing the gist of a long passage read out by the examiner), and spoken German.

There was a break for lunch after the first two sessions.

Before the recess each candidate was told when to report for the final part.

I did not take any chances and returned to the examination hall in good time for my turn.

One after the other, those ahead of me were called into a comparatively smaller adjacent room for the oral test. Some emerged about ten minutes later showing no emotion; others smiled their joys while a few openly talked about their disappointment for not having made it.

Just before it was my turn, a young lady with European features was called into the examination room. About ten minutes later, she burst out of the room into the larger hall, weeping uncontrollably.

'Please, help me!' she pleaded. 'I cannot return to Poland, please! I hate the Communists! Please have mercy on me!' (Readers might recall that in 1984 Poland was in turmoil with the Solidarity Movement battling it out with the Communist regime.)

She cried so loud that one of the examiners was prompted to come out of the room to try and console her. It was a pitiful sight to behold.

For a moment, the scene unfolding around me threatened to unsettle me.

'No way!' I said to myself. 'The stakes are too high to allow myself to be overcome by emotions!' Taking a deep breath, I mustered all the strength I could gather and waited for my turn.

Finally I was called in.

'How and where did you learn the German language?' one of the panel members inquired.

Though I did not boast the best spoken German, I made use of the little knowledge I commanded to briefly narrate the steps I had taken so far to acquire my knowledge.

A few more questions followed, centred on why I wanted to study medicine and also how I was coping with my new environment.

Next I was asked to wait outside while the panel deliberated on my performance. A few minutes later, I was called back into the room. Shortly after I was seated, the chairman smiled at me and began:

'The panel has reached the conclusion that you deserve the chance to take up your studies. There is however room for improvement. In this regard we recommend that whenever your schedule at the medical school permits, you attend the free German lesson classes offered by the university to foreign students.' I was then handed my certificate. With it, I was able, finally, to realise my goal of studying medicine.

PART FOUR
FINAL REFLECTIONS

34
ONE THING BEING ADMITTED TO MEDICAL SCHOOL: ANOTHER THING QUALIFYING AS A DOCTOR !

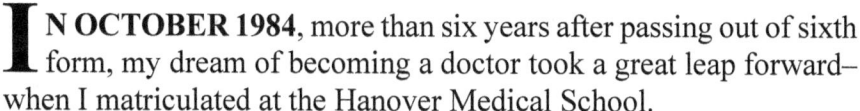

IN OCTOBER 1984, more than six years after passing out of sixth form, my dream of becoming a doctor took a great leap forward– when I matriculated at the Hanover Medical School.

'Congratulations on your achievement', one might want to declare with a pat on my shoulders.

Well, that would be premature, my friend, for the real battle had only just begun!

It is definitely one thing entering a medical school; it is completely a different thing passing out as a doctor.

Between my first day at medical school and my passing out as a doctor lay several years of hard work, hard work and, once again, hard work! There were volumes and volumes of material I had to learn in various subjects: anatomy, biochemistry, physiology, pathology, neurology, dermatology, surgery, etc.

On not a few occasions, when on the day prior to an important examination I had spent several hours of the day revising my notes only to realise towards the latter part of the day there was still a great deal of material that I still needed to go through before the dawn of the next day, I paused for a while to reflect on the whole concept of examinations as we have it now.

Why has our civilisation not come up with any other method of testing the individual's knowledge in their areas of study, rather than resort to methods that may well be described as bordering on mental torture? So long as no alternative has been developed, however, one has no other choice but to play by the rules.

It is not an exercise without reward, however. For example, in my work as a doctor I am often presented with a prescription, a note or a document already prepared by a nurse, a health care assistant or another health care worker to sign.

Though the persons involved might be equally well informed about the medication or the document in question, they are legally constrained from signing. What makes the difference between me and them? My medical certificate, the certificate I 'tortured' my mind to obtain!

35
AS FAR AS IT DEPENDS ON US, LET'S BE ON GOOD TERMS WITH ALL

IN OUR JOURNEY to the attainment of our goal, as far as it lies with us, we need to strive to be on good terms with all.

Sadly we live in a world not devoid of tribalism, racism, nationalism, religious intolerance, etc. My native Ghana is made up of several different tribes. Just because one belongs to a different tribe can result in one being rejected at an interview. Then there's the issue of skin colour, sex, nationality, political and religious affiliation, etc.

Tribalism, racism, nationalism, and what have you, will never be completely eliminated from an imperfect world. If we are to wait until such imperfect traits of humanity are completely eradicated from the surface of the earth before we seek to interact with others who are different from us, that time will never come.

As I mentioned earlier, my desire to find a church where I could worship on my arrival in West Berlin led me to the American Church in Berlin. At the time I joined the church, I was the only African in a congregation made up, apart from a few Indians, almost completely of individuals of European descent.

Someone in the same position as I was may have been reluctant to turn up the following Sunday. I returned, nevertheless, and remained there throughout my stay in the divided city.

Though I did not go there with the primary purpose of gaining favour from anyone, my association with the congregation brought countless blessings. When I finally took up my studies two years later, the financial assistance of the church, especially in the early years of my study, proved vital.

I would never have realised my goal of becoming a doctor without what I describe as the 'German connection'. I profited not only from the German welfare system, which in particular helped fix the problem of my left ankle, but also benefitted from the free tuition offered me by a German university.

Beside the German state, I also received invaluable help, both financial and material from German nationals such as Anna, Gottfried, Ilse, Kurt, Rhea, Ruth – the list seems endless.

Indeed, in my journey to the fulfilment of my goal, I received more help from Germans and others of European descent than citizens of my own country.

I am not implying that I did not face some degree of racial prejudice and discrimination along the way. I was however so focussed on my goal, that I did not allow myself to be distracted by the negative attitude or behaviour of others towards me.

36
LET'S BE WARY OF DISTRACTIONS!

LET US IMAGINE you are an ardent football lover. A day before your final exams, your team is involved in a very special game. What do you do?

Whatever your decision, one thing should be paramount. Your team, unless they go financially bankrupt, will keep on playing games. Your examinations on the other hand may be a once-in-alifetime opportunity to shine.

This brings me to the subject of distractions – yes, the things that take our attention away from what we are supposed to be doing.

Apart from impediments that may come our way, indeed, events and occurrences over which we have no control, we are sure to face distractions of various kinds.

At the time I was working towards the achievement of my goal, the world had not made much headway in information technology.

For the most part of the period under consideration, my communication with family members, friends, and others was mainly by way of writing letters and also talking on the phone. In regard to the phone, the network in Ghana was so underdeveloped that it was unavailable in many parts of the country. Needless to say, there was no way I could pick up the phone at the boarding school to communicate with my parents.

As a teenager and later a young adult, other forms of distraction came from my friends and peers – listening to music, partying, attending disco, watching TV. I was so focussed on realising my goal, however, that I was determined not to allow anything to sidetrack me.

When I was at medical school, the only thing that could distract me was the TV in my room – not that I had the inclination to watch for long. Still, it could be a source of distraction. In the critical period when exams were being written, even giving way to watching TV for a few minutes, as far as I was concerned, was too much. What did I do? I just left my room and spent the time in the library.

Much has happened in the world since the events recorded in this book. In 1995 a friend of mine, also a Ghanaian studying at a town not far from Hanover, paid me a visit. During his stay he presented me with several sheets of paper which happened to be print-outs of current happenings in Ghana.

'How did you come across such 'hot' news items from home?' I wanted to know.

'From the Internet,' was his reply.

'The Internet? What is that?' I inquired in amazement.

'It is a network of computers', he began. 'It enables the spread of information throughout the globe. We currently rely on it a great deal in my field of study – mining engineering.'

I need not bore readers with any further details concerning the Internet. Much has indeed happened in our world since the Internet made its appearance. With the help of my visitor, I set up my first e-mail account in 1995!

The age of the Internet has arrived, and mobile phones, smart phones, iPhones, iPads – you name them – are indeed here to stay.

I must admit that on not a few occasions each day, being the grey-haired old-fashioned fellow that I am, I feel overwhelmed and powerless before the rapidly evolving *monster* that goes by the name of information technology.

I really do wonder how other members of the human race, especially the youth, are managing to cope with the flood of information unleashed on them from the millions of departments of the cyber establishment – Facebook, *headbook*, Twitter, *twatter*, YouTube, *you tunnel*…you can go on naming them indefinitely!

I am not calling for the clock of time to be turned backwards to the time when the world was devoid of the internet. Admittedly, the revolution in information technology has brought with it several advantages.

Despite the huge advantage it has brought, especially for academic life, the student should not lose sight of its serious potential for distraction.

Internet or no Internet, one thing has not changed in academic life – the need not only to pass our examinations, but to pass them in order to be able to compete with our peers in an increasingly competitive world.

The bottom line should be – am I spending more time on the Internet, my iPhone, my PlayStation, etc., than pursuing the steps towards the achievement of my goal?

37
OTHERS JUMPING ON OUR BANDWAGON OF SUCCESS

IN AUGUST 1984, I faced the real threat of deportation from Germany back to Ghana. If that had happened, this would have been my situation:

1) I would have been sent back to Ghana empty-handed.
    It is no secret that people in Ghana and elsewhere in the developing world look to the West as a kind of heaven on earth. Everyone there who was aware of my whereabouts, family members, friends, schoolmates, etc., would have expected that having spent some time in *Aburokyire* (the term used in Ghana for the Western industrialised world), I would be returning home with abundant wealth. (The fact that I spent only a little over two years in Europe would have made little difference to them.)
    Returning home with nothing by way of material wealth to show, would have subjected me to ridicule.
2) My educational career would have been in shambles – I would have spent six years struggling to be admitted to medical school only to end up with nothing! What would I have told

my schoolmates – from elementary school, Oda Secondary School and Mfantsipim School on meeting them on the streets of Accra, Oda, Cape Coast and elsewhere in the country? Happily, I was spared that fate.

During the time that I was struggling to make ends meet in Germany, I communicated sporadically with my family back home. Though I received some letters with requests for financial assistance from some members of the family, I had little choice but to neglect them.

Though I did not immediately inform relatives and friends back home about my admission to medical school, a time came when I felt the need to do so.

Soon word went round to the effect that I had made it to medical school in Germany of all places! Soon, everyone wanted to share in my glory.

At the time when in Nigeria I carried concrete on my head, from one floor to another, limping on my ailing leg, or at the time when I faced a real threat of deportation, indeed at the time when my six-year effort to get to medical school was in seeming shambles, my whole world seemed to have collapsed.

But let us also beware when, after all the struggles to reach our goal, we finally make it! While this phenomena is not peculiar to a developing country such as Ghana, the widespread poverty in Ghana and other developing countries, coupled with the fact that there is hardly if any state benefit system in place in such societies, makes the situation even more pronounced.

In most rich western countries, the state makes it a responsibility to cater for the disadvantaged of society. Many living in such societies may express their displeasure with their governments for the inadequacy of the system. At least their governments, however, are making the effort. The situation is different in a society like Ghana. There, for various reasons that are beyond the remit of this book to delve into, there is no such state-supported benefit system. The responsibility falls upon members of the extended family.

In the midst of scores struggling to survive, anyone who in the eyes of family members is making headway in life becomes a focus of attention – looked upon by the rest to provide much needed financial assistance, notwithstanding the fact that the individual involved may also have his or her own peculiar problems.

Though I have done my best to meet their expectations, even as I write I am not sure everyone is satisfied with my efforts.

38
SO HOW DO WE BEAT THE ODDS TO SUCCESS?

In conclusion, I want to stress that I know no easy ways to beat the odds to success other than through hard work, perseverance, sheer will-power and personal responsibility. We should not depend on chance, on opportunities dropped from the sky. While opportunity may favour our progress, exertion is indispensable; indeed, at the end of the day, there is nothing good, great or desirable that does not come by way of some kind of labour.

We should refrain from seeking short cuts to success; we may also waste valuable time idling by the shore waiting for our ship to come in. We should not count on luck, on chance, on winning the jackpot to see us through life. You might as well spend time whistling in the wind!

Instead, we should seize the initiative, and work towards the realisation of our goal. We will surely face obstacles, difficulties, disappointments along the way. That, however, should not deter us from persevering. No matter the circumstances, with hard work, determination, steadfastness, self-discipline and keeping a clear purpose or goal in view, I believe from my personal experience that we will be destined to succeed, no matter how long it takes us.

As we labour on towards the attainment of our goal the following points may bring us inspiration and comfort in times of distress and uncertainty:

- Even when everyone seems to have given up on us we should not give up on ourselves; indeed, we should be the last person to give up on our dreams!
- Even if we seem to be receiving a merciless whipping in the boxing ring of life, even if a heavy punch to the face has sent us tumbling to floor, so long as the referee has not finally counted us out, let's muster the very little energy remaining in us and strive to get back on our feet!
- Even if everyone around is urging us to quit for lack of prospect of success, we should stay our course; yes, we should make the resolve not to be counted among the quitters!
- Even when our legs are bruised and hurting in the marathon of life, let's draw inspiration from the likes of John Stephen Akhwari, and keep on running; for indeed, we joined in the race not only for the sake of joining, but for the sake of finishing! Indeed, let's keep on running the race of life with determination, whatever the odds are.
- Let us not allow perceived disadvantages, be it our social background, sex, skin colour, race, whatever, to be an excuse for not trying to aim at achieving high laurels in life! In as much as others before us, who have shared our perceived impairments, have made it, we can as well. So let us not give up with the excuse that we are the helpless victim of circumstances. Let us get up and get to work!!
- We should also desist from magnifying the perceived negatives. Instead we should concentrate on the positives.
- Finally... If the author of these lines, despite starting his academic journey from an impoverished primary school in

a remote village in Africa, ended up rubbing shoulders with medical students at the prestigious Hanover Medical School in Germany, one of the leading industrialised countries on earth, you too, dear reader, can achieve similar and even greater feats, no matter your starting point in life – be it in the slums of Sodom and Gomorrah in Accra, Ghana; Manila in the Philippines; Calcutta in India; Rio de Janeiro in Brazil... you can keep on naming all the disadvantaged spots and locations of our imperfect planet until the cows come home!

So I urge you to get up and start running, you who are burying your head in the sand, thinking there is no way out of your misery! Yes, be brave and do not lose heart! Head up and not head down, friend; look up, not down!! Yes, be of good cheer, friend, for you really can. Yes, you can!!

* * *

Before I finally close this last chapter of my book, I want to cite examples of three historical figures who, through hard work and perseverance, managed to beat the odds to success. In going through the biographies of these and several other historical figures who rose from their disadvantaged positions to accomplish something in their respective spheres of human endeavour, it became clear to me that such individuals were men and women of hard work and that the best, if not the only, explanation of their success was honest labour faithfully, steadily and persistently pursued.

Marie Curie, 1867–1934

Marie Curie was a Polish and naturalised French physicist and chemist who conducted pioneering research on radioactivity.

At the time of her birth on November 7, 1867 in central Warsaw, Poland was then a subject state of Russia and women were excluded from advanced study. Not prepared to be handicapped by the odds, she left her native Poland in 1891 to join her sister Bronia in Paris. On arrival in France, she enrolled at the Paris Sorbonne University.

Through hard work, sheer determination and obsessive dedication to scientific research, Marie Curie went on to discover the elements polonium and radium.

In 1903 she became the first female to be awarded the Nobel Prize, when she shared the Nobel Prize for physics with her husband and another researcher for their work on radiation. In 1911 she became the first person (and only woman) to win twice when she received the Nobel Prize for Chemistry.

Frederick Douglass, 1818–1895

'Allowing for only ordinary ability and opportunity, we may explain success mainly by one word and that word is WORK! WORK!! WORK!!! WORK!!!!'

Through tenacity and passion, Frederick rose from the shackles of slavery to extraordinary success. Born a slave, Frederick Douglass was not permitted any form of education. His master's wife, who had attempted to teach him the alphabet, had to give up her efforts when she was reprimanded for doing so by her husband.

Not deterred, Frederick continued to learn by interacting with white children and working through any written materials he could find.

In 1838, he took his greatest risk yet by escaping from slavery.

He soon rose to prominence, becoming an outspoken abolitionist, and consul-general to the Republic of Haiti, and chargé d'affaires for the Dominican Republic.

During the 1888 Republican Convention, he became the first African-American to receive a vote to be nominated for the Presidency.

At the time of his death in 1895, Douglass had risen from slavery to become one of the most prominent and well-respected black men in the United States.

Abraham Lincoln, 1809–1865

'Things may come to those who wait, but only the things left by those who hustle.'

Though he lacked connections, charisma, good looks, and formal education, Abraham Lincoln ended up becoming one of the greatest presidents in the history of the United States.

Born in a one-room cabin to uneducated farmer parents, he received only 18 months of formal education. In the end he was almost entirely self-educated. Teaching himself law, he rose up to become a successful attorney and state legislator in Illinois.

In 1860 he was elected the 16th President of the USA. Lincoln led the United States through its civil war and, in doing so, he preserved the Union, abolished slavery, strengthened the federal government, and modernised the economy.

These examples show that the only way to succeed is through hard work and not giving up!

www.ingramcontent.com/pod-product-compliance
Lightning Source LLC
Chambersburg PA
CBHW070507100426
42743CB00010B/1782